The Toolbox for Building a Great Family Dog

Terry Ryan

Dogwise™ Publishing
Wenatchee, WA

The Toolbox for Building a Great Family Dog
Terry Ryan

Dogwise Publishing
A Division of Direct Book Service, Inc.
403 South Mission Street, Wenatchee, Washington 98801
509-663-9115, 1-800-776-2665
www.dogwisepublishing.com / info@dogwisepublishing.com

Graphic design: Lindsay Peternell
Illustrations: Elaine Diedrich, Jackie McCowen

Some of this content has previously appeared in *The Toolbox for Remodeling Your Problem Dog, The Bark Stops Here* and *Coaching People to Train Their Dogs.* Used with permission from Terry Ryan

Limits of Liability and Disclaimer of Warranty:
The author and publisher shall not be liable in the event of incidental or consequential damages in connection with, or arising out of, the furnishing, performance, or use of the instructions and suggestions contained in this book.

ISBN 978-1929242-795

Library of Congress Cataloging-in-Publication Data

Ryan, Terry, 1946 Mar. 5-
    The toolbox for building a great family dog / Terry Ryan.
        p. cm.
    Includes index.
    ISBN 978-1-929242-79-5
    1. Dogs--Training. I. Title.
    SF431.R9349 2010
    636.7'0887--dc22

                                            2010041139

Printed in the U.S.A.

To Gus, a special agility dog.

More praise for *The Toolbox for Building a Great Family Dog*

I remember Terry's original Toolbox from way back when—us newbie trainers considered it the gospel! It was a succinct, practical guide for pet owners. I sat down to peruse the new, revised and expanded Toolbox and DID NOT PUT IT DOWN UNTIL I WAS FINISHED! It is an outstanding guide for dog people.

What consistently impresses me about Terry is her relentless determination to make training and behavior modification fit the needs of everyday pet owner. Terry has been an icon in the dog-training field since before I entered it in 1981, and is one of the most influential dog trainers ever. Never stale, never outdated, never ignorant of all the new developments in dog training and behavior. And she incorporates all the knowledge she gathers: drawing from biology, ethology, learning theory, wolves, chickens, dogs living in a dump in Mexico City—you name it. The result is a book filled with the best advice an owner could ask for.

The Feng Shui of Terry's brain is pure and healthy. She is able to organize all her vast knowledge into an efficient, tidy, uncluttered, relevant and useful book.

This book is as much a relationship-builder as it is a training manual. The exercises in the book inspires a dog-human partnership that is healthy, clear, humane and, most importantly, successful.

Sue Sternberg, author of *Serious Fun, Out and About With Your Dog, Successful Dog Adoption,* and a host of DVDs on dog behavior. www.suesternberg.com.

Okay, I'll admit it. After readingTerry Ryan's *The Toolbox for Building a Great Family Dog* I just had to go to my bookshelf and dig up some of her previous books. Sure enough, this "Toolbox" combines new knowledge with tried and true advice from not just one, but three of Ryan's classic releases. She has honored the flavor and structure of her previous work while infusing it with new energy and knowledge.

Simply put, this book is not only going on my bookshelf, it will be on my recommended reading list for new clients and K9 handlers.

Steve White, Police K9 Trainer

TABLE OF CONTENTS

INTRODUCTION

I didn't plan to write this book. It sort of evolved on its own. Its predecessor, *The Toolbox for Remodeling Your Problem Dog* was published by Howell Book House in 1998. It was simply a documentation of what I was doing to help clients change inappropriate behavior in their pet dogs. It's been out of print for years. When Dogwise Publishing asked if they could reprint it, I hesitated, but eventually said yes. I explained, "It's old, give me a while, it needs tweaking. I'm not doing things exactly that way now-a-days."

Well, the tweaking turned into a major rewrite. One thing led to another. There was a lot I wasn't doing any more, including waiting for "problems" to happen and then trying to "fix" them. I've taken a much more proactive attitude in the last decade, developing new puppy programs and pet dog foundation exercises to try to circumvent the "problems" people have been talking to me about for the last forty-something years.

The "new" *Toolbox* emphasizes setting the stage to allow a great pet to happen. It focuses on building a relationship with your dog, the home environment and life styles, in addition to training basic manners. You will see that I place particular emphasis on providing the proper home environment when it comes to living with a family dog. The chapter titles I've chosen build a link between constructing a home and training a dog—from making plans, to understanding the use of the materials, to building a foundation, and so on all the way up to the finishing touches.

It's an exciting time to be involved in dog training. Change is happening. Opinions, trends, and in some cases, even some of the science and terminology has changed since I got started. I've dropped several terms from my vocabulary. Little by little I'm phasing out terms like "leadership" and "social hierarchy." These are valid concepts, but they are often interpreted and portrayed in ways that I personally feel are—to be blunt—not good for dogs, not beneficial for people, and not helpful for society in general.

In the early1960s, when I first attempted to collect the complete dog training library, there were less than ten books (in English) on the topic. Now there seem to be ten different TV shows on training, let alone scores of new books, magazines, DVDs, internet lists, on-line seminars, and a growing variety of types of training equipment. How do we sort through all of this in the name of humane and effective dog training?

Well, one thing has remained constant and true. The experts have the real information. Those experts are the dogs. While it would be easier for us if dogs could talk, fortunately they do use a language—body language—the principal way in which they communicate. I have learned how to read at least some of what they express. So far, I've just accumulated many more questions about dogs than answers, but some things are falling into place. I've learned to take a multi-disciplinary approach in my attempt to understand and train dogs. Veterinarians, biologists, psychologists, ethologists, and many others outside of the dog training field have helped me realize the importance of the many independent variables you must consider to get close to understanding what makes each individual dog tick.

Let's first learn about the basic building blocks required to help construct a great family dog.

Chapter 1

THE RAW MATERIAL

YOUR DOG'S BEHAVIOR

Understanding your dog's behavior will make you a better trainer.

Many people think about dog training the same way they think about driving a car. "I just want to get into the driver's seat and drive. I don't want to know all about what's going on under the hood." Just learning to steer, brake, and accelerate might be okay—until something goes wrong that requires knowing more than how to turn the key and step on the gas pedal. I believe it's the same with dogs. It helps to understand the inner workings of dogs if you are going to be able to train them effectively and coexist with them happily.

Fortunately, behavioral research is being conducted that is useful for dog trainers. Verifiable data about behavior can help trainers learn how to formulate better training plans. However, even more fact-finding needs to be done to find out what really makes dogs tick. Too often trainers—including myself—have to supplement the known facts with our own experience and anecdotal information. Here are some key behavioral concepts that you should think about before attempting to train your dog.

The anthropomorphism trap

Dogs and people are similar in many ways. But there are some clear differences as well. Can dogs think? Do dogs have emotions? It all depends on the definition or interpretation of the word "think" or "emotion." Dogs do have a range of feelings, but they probably don't equate exactly to our own emotions. Dogs can acquire, process, and store information, but in their own way.

When people don't recognize the differences between how humans and dogs acquire and process information, they might resort to anthropomorphism (assigning human motivation and behavior to animals). While it may make you feel like you know what is going on, it doesn't do much good in terms of understanding and influencing your dog's behavior. Many times I've heard people say, "He peed on the rug to get even with me." There are so many more logical reasons this happened—reasons that come with a built-in fix. He drank too much water, he's on meds, he became frightened, he's sick, or he doesn't completely understand your toilet training attempts. "He loves me" is a concept that is dear to many of us. Your dog might love you and certainly you can love him back, but having the opposable thumbs to work can openers doesn't hurt either. You are even more loveable because you can turn door knobs, start the car, make toys play back, and give invitations to share great resting places with electric blankets.

Your dog has a variety of reasons to dig: Find a cool place, bury something, dig something up. Recreational digging is something to expend energy on, not to get "even" with you. It is not enough to say your dog is digging holes. How many reasons can you come up with for a dog to want to dig holes? The specific reason should guide your choice of behavior modification tools.

Learning about a dog's point of view

You will gain more insight into the training process by looking at life from a different point of view—your dog's. Dogs are contextual learners. This means that they are heavily influenced by the context or situation in which things occur. This can be a problem for humans because, while we may think we are training one thing, the dog is actually learning something else.

Here is an example showing the importance of context. Greta and her person, Ed, are going for a walk. Greta launches herself at a cat, pulling the leash out of Ed's hand. Greta is already in the street when Ed shouts, "Greta! *BAD!*" What did Greta learn from this experience? We don't know for sure, but here are some possibilities:

1. She learned Ed disapproves of her chasing cats.

2. She's so focused on the chase, she doesn't even hear Ed's reprimand, and so learns nothing from Ed.

3. She was near a mailbox at the time and has learned to avoid mailboxes. She associates them with Ed's angry outbursts.

4. She thinks Ed is upset that she was too slow and didn't catch the cat.

5. She thinks Ed is cheering her on.

6. _____ (you fill in the blank…)

As in Greta's cat chasing incident, there are times when the context of a learned behavior is irrelevant to the owner, but key to the dog. Either way, she is learning something from her environment.

Here's another example. Eight-week old Lacey, an English Cocker Spaniel, arrived at our house late one October. It was an unusually snowy winter. We began to teach Lacey, as we had all of our other dogs, to sit by the door as a way to indicate that someone should let her out to potty. All seemed to be going well with her housetraining, except on days when it was actually snowing. On those days, Lacey would sit to be let out as usual to the designated toilet area in the back yard, but instead of walking off the deck to the proper spot, she would potty right on the deck. The family began to call it the Poop Deck. I needed to get to the bottom of this. Remember, she only did this when fresh snow was falling. On those days the deck was completely covered with snow—just like the back yard! However, when the deck was clear of snow, she would head right to the yard.

After thinking hard about this, I realized that I thought I was rewarding Lacey for toileting in a *certain location,* but that's not what she learned. What she had actually learned was to potty on a *certain type of surface*—snow! Each time it snowed and covered the deck, in her mind the deck was then fair game. On days when the deck was clear, she would step off into the yard like a good girl…in search of snow. Lacey's association was "on snow," not "over here," as I thought I was teaching her.

THE POOP DECK

I inadvertently taught Lacey to relieve herself on snow instead of a specific part of the yard.

Oh, in case you were wondering, when spring finally arrived and the snow started to disappear, Lacey went further and further into the shady parts of the yard to find some snow. She eventually figured out that she didn't really need snow after all.

Nature and nurture

As with humans, a dog's behavior is the result of his genetic predisposition (nature) interacting with his life experiences (nurture). The concept of nature versus nurture is deceiving in that behavior can not be traced to one or the other exclusively. Nature and nurture effects are synergistic. They work together and can not be separated into totally distinct categories. Some natural behaviors, which we happen to find problematic to our lifestyle choices, are simply the dog's attempt at satisfying instinctual demands. Think of a hound chasing a rabbit or a terrier digging a hole. These are normal, instinctive behaviors for these dogs, but of course chasing and digging behaviors don't always fit in with a pet owner's lifestyle.

When assessing your dog's behavior and how you will go about training him, consider the nature and nurture issue. You may train your dog to do one thing, but nature is whispering another. We have a coop full of chickens at our training center. Our dog Brody is also at the center every day. He's conditioned to pretty much ignore the chickens. However, Brody is an English Cocker Spaniel. I'm not going to bet the well-being of my chickens on my ability as a trainer. Not with that little bird dog. Supervision and management must take precedence.

Sensitive periods in a dog's development

A dog's behavior is shaped largely by the experiences he has as a puppy, a process referred to as *socialization*. Think of a puppy's brain as having lots of little electrical plugs and sockets floating in space. What connects them properly are *triggers* or *precursors*—events that the dog experiences that influence his behavior. There are optimal windows of opportunity for these mental connections to be made. Most of these critical periods occur before sixteen weeks of age. The onset and offset of these periods vary from puppy to puppy and can be as short as a couple of weeks. That is why what happens early in life can so profoundly influence a dog's future behavior.

A well-run puppy class will concentrate on providing useful learning and socialization experiences for very young dogs. I highly recommend you enroll your puppy in one. If your pup does not get the appropriate experiences during these critical periods, it is more difficult for him to reach full potential as a well-adjusted adult. I am writing an entire book on puppy training and socialization prompted by recent research of brain development in dogs. If you have, or plan to add, a puppy to your family, please learn more about these important early days in a pup's life.

A well run puppy program helps you build a well adjusted dog.

A socialization program is different from a pet dog manners class, although such a class does help socialize your pup to some degree. Rather than concentrating on specific behaviors such as Sit, Down or Heel, a socialization program focuses on exposing a puppy to a variety of life's experiences (other dogs, people, noises, etc.) in a way that the puppy will be comfortable with them. You should think of it as a relationship program for your dog with the entire world. With guidance, this is something you can do on your own outside of a class setting. If your dog is over sixteen weeks of age, have you missed your chance to influence her? No, but just like a child that has missed kindergarten and first grade, concepts need to be taught that would have been more easily learned at an earlier age.

Social hierarchy: What it is, what it is not

Here are commonly heard pieces of advice given to dog owners: "You need to be the alpha," or "You must be the dominant pack leader." Analogies to wolf packs and human families and how to simulate "natural" canine pack order abound. Don't believe everything you hear, read on-line, or see on television. Be a critical thinker. Superficial appearance of a method "working" does not mean that it's really effective or that it is the best method for you and your dog. Nor can you be sure that it won't have future detrimental effects.

Studies by experts in the field of canine behavior show that interactions between dogs are much more flexible than those advocates of strict hierarchies assert. A dog can adopt a "dominant" or a "subordinate" stance depending on the situation, but it does not mean he is stuck forever in that role. If you carefully watch dogs and puppies play, you will see that they will sometimes switch back and forth between dominant or subordinate postures. The same dog can be seen trying out one or the other at different times, reflecting the relationship at that moment in time.

"It depends." Those are the two words I'd use if forced to sum up social hierarchy in dogs. It is affected by independent variables such as context and the physical state of the dog and those around him. One dog might be able to dominate others when it comes to resting places, but that individual might freely yield food to others. A dog may guard food only if hungry, or if it's a particularly yummy, high value treat. Once again, it depends.

I learned some valuable lessons at a dump in Mexico City. Led by evolutionary biologist Dr. Ray Coppinger, we spent a week observing and documenting canine behavior and how dogs adapt to their environment. The dump is huge and home to hundreds of dogs. What we saw was, rather than dogs trying to dominate each other, they mostly tried to *avoid* getting into fights. We were amazed at how well their conflict avoidance skills worked. We saw very few dog fights and few overt threatening behaviors, even though the dogs had to compete for resources like water and shade. They seemed to have found a way to avoid most conflicts. My guess is that the dogs had worked out the cost/benefit of using up large amounts of energy on such behaviors—using them only when they are absolutely necessary.

Something to keep in mind is that there is more room in the world for subordinate individuals than dominant ones. Therefore, ranking of individuals in a social living group might more accurately be described as a *subordinance hierarchy* than a *dominance hierarchy*. It's always better to talk about what you *see* a dog doing rather than *labeling* it with a more-than-likely ambiguous or anthropomorphic term.

Dominance ≠ Aggression

These terms, as popularly used, are not the same. Dominance is based on social ranking with others. Aggression is based on an individual's state of mind, usually involving a valued resource. A dog can be aggressive, but not dominant, or dominant, but not aggressive—or a dog can be both.

The alpha roll

The *alpha roll* is a technique shown in an assortment of literature and media. There seems to be no standard definition of the alpha roll; in fact, there are many variations demonstrated by trainers. One variation starts with grabbing the dog on either side of the neck, lifting the dog's weight off his or her front feet, perhaps shaking him up a little and staring into the dog's eyes. Next, is turning the dog onto his back and pinning him on the floor until he submits to what is thought to be an effective display of "dominance" and "pack leadership." However, there is usually no clear definition given of the terms dominance, pack leadership, or submission. Nor is there an explanation of what to do if the dog doesn't submit. This forced, violent action under the guise of pack leadership can result in the human sustaining a physical injury and doing the dog psychological harm. It should leave us wondering what the dog actually learned.

Why do trainers show dog owners the alpha roll? It is purported to simulate the natural method of establishing leadership, dominating the dog, correcting a dog, punishing an inappropriate behavior. Definitions and critical thinking are called for. Some trainers justify the technique of the alpha roll because it's "nature's way." It's the way wolves do it. Do they have data to back up their statement? Have they ever personally observed wolves? Probably not. This information has been handed down over the years. I've had the glorious opportunity to observe wolves numerous times. My observations taught me just enough to know all the things I don't know and never will know about the social dynamics of wolves. I was left with more questions than answers. But I do know there are better ways to provide leadership for your dog than pinning him on his back until he submits.

Here is what the American Veterinary Society of Animal Behavior says about this issue:

> AVSAB is concerned with the recent re-emergence of dominance theory and forcing dogs and other animals into submission as a means of preventing and correcting behavior problems. For decades, some traditional animal training has relied on dominance theory and has assumed that animals misbehave primarily because they are striving for higher rank. This idea often leads trainers to believe that force or coercion must be used to modify these undesirable behaviors. In the last several decades, our understanding of dominance theory and of the behavior of domesticated animals and their wild counterparts has grown considerably, leading to updated views.

The body language of dogs

One thing we know for sure is that dogs are masters of body language. This natural method of communication might not be readily apparent to humans. Canine body language is too complex for simple explanations. The displays are many and varied, some of the signals are subtle and ambiguous. The following pages will help you understand what your dog is trying to say.

Some types of body language displays are quickly and easily recognized by most people. I think of these gestures and postures as CAPITAL LETTERS in **bold print**. There are other displays and signals that are more subtle and might be easily overlooked. I think of those as lower case letters or fine print. These signals act as an "early warning" system. We don't have to wait for the dog to shout, we know that something is up if we pay attention to the precursors, the whispers.

Body language used for conflict resolution

Of particular importance to owners and trainers of family dogs are the aspects of body language that relate to conflict avoidance or resolution. It is now a well-established fact that dogs use body language to signal each other in an effort to avoid conflict. The better we humans can recognize what a dog is trying to communicate, the easier it is for us to live together "happily ever after."

Baseline posture

The baseline posture depicted below is of a middle-of-the-road dog. Not too bold, not too worried, a dog who is probably pretty easy to be around. When a dog is relaxed, his or her entire body shows that relaxation. The muscles are fluid and the dog moves gracefully. Compare this baseline to the following drawings and descriptions to see how postures and expressions change depending on the mental state of the dog.

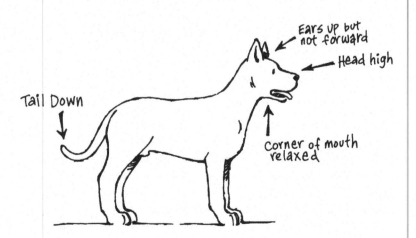

Relaxed baseline or body posture.

Offensive displays

Here is a dog displaying offensive body language appearing fearless, assertive, and self-confident. Like a fullback on a football team, this dog is out to score. He appears to be the one trying to call the shots, the one commanding the situation, the one asking the interloper to back down or suffer the consequences.

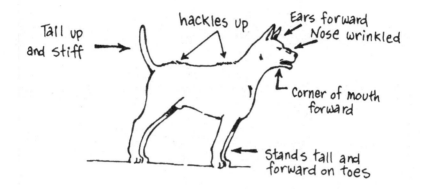

Offensive body posture.

The posture of an offensive dog appears to make the animal larger than he really is. In general, the body appears to be up and forward from the dog's neutral body profile. When a dog is aroused, his body becomes tight—the mouth, the large muscles, all the way down to the dog's legs. What you see is a more rigid, than flexible, dog. In general, the offensively threatening dog faces a problem straight on. The hackles (hair) along the back of the dog may be raised. The tail might be elevated higher than the neutral position and wagging slowly. The base of the ears will be up and forward. The dog makes eye contact with the interloper. The dog may show his teeth, growl, or bark. Challenge the dog and he might lunge, chase, or bite if given the opportunity.

Fortunately, there are few truly offensive dogs. Rehabilitation of an offensive dog is beyond the scope of this book. If you believe your dog is behaving offensively, ask your veterinarian for a referral to a behavior consultant. It is more likely that your dog's actions fall into the defensive category.

Hackles

Any type of arousal can produce raised hackles (piloerection). Examples include a dog who hears a strange sound, a dog who is greeting another, or a dog having a romp with a friend. Usually the hair along the spine comes up, but the piloerection can include hair all the way from the forehead to the tail.

Defensive displays

Here is a dog displaying defensive body language. He looks the opposite of the offensive dog. He will be low to the ground as if to protect the vulnerable parts of his body. His hackles may be up. Defensive dogs usually avoid direct eye contact. The ears and tail will be down and the dog adopts a backward leaning posture. A defensive dog may growl and bark, or whine, or just be quiet. He may take a little lunge forward, but then back up. If an intruder is "chased" away, the defensive dog will often withdraw his threat.

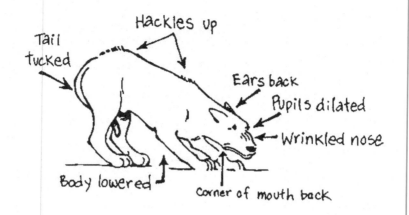

Defensive body posture.

Although the actions of a defensive dog may be misinterpreted as threatening, these actions are based on fear. Beneath the surface, the dog is actually hesitant, nervous, and distrustful. The owner of this dog may think, "He's protecting me," but the dog is actually standing behind the owner, hoping for help to get rid of whatever is scaring him. If the defensive dog feels threatened and has no way to retreat, he might lash out.

The shield and spear analogy
In the old days, human conflict resolution sometimes involved people with shields and spears. Think of your dog as carrying a mental shield and spear. If he uses the spear, he is being offensive—the unabashed challenger ready to attack others. If he uses the shield, he's defensive—fending off the enemy or trying to escape harm. However, the shield carrier may change tactics. If in a position where the shield or escape isn't working, he might strike out in an attempt to get rid of the perceived threat.

Conflict resolution—Submission
Submissive displays are shown toward people or dogs in an attempt to establish or acknowledge a relationship. As illustrated below, submissive displays can either be active or passive. The dog will usually have his ears laid back and his tail down. He will appear to be almost groveling in his movements. Some submissive gestures are similar to those meant to communicate anxiety (fear, stress). Gestures of lower rank are not necessarily signals of fear. An overly submissive dog can pose a training problem. Positive methods and a change in relationship are in order and can be very effective in training this dog.

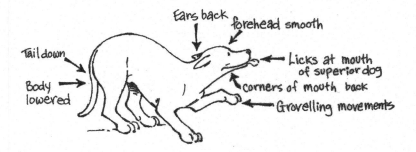

Active submission: Friendly, but polite greeting posture, showing deference.

Passive submission: Worried, extreme greeting posture, showing surrender.

Ambivalence

The ambivalent dog is unsure, unclear, undecided and the body postures might show both offensive and defensive components at the same time. In the end, it may depend on the way the other dog (or person) responds to determine if the dog will act offensively or defensively.

Calming signals

Sometimes, rather than adopting an all out offensive or defensive display, dogs will choose to resolve a potential conflict by displaying more subtle behaviors which can "turn off" or inhibit perceived threats from others. These acts of pacification or reconciliation are often referred to by some canine professionals as *appeasement*, others refer to part or all of them as *calming signals*. Ethologists sometimes label similar or same displays as *cut-off signals*.

Much of our knowledge of these types of behaviors is a result of the work of Norwegian dog specialist Turid Rugaas. Turid is credited with coining the term "calming signals." She explains calming signals as visual cues that produce pacifying effects on the dog exhibiting them and toward the individual at whom they are aimed. Turid believes that these signals often curtail hostilities before they have a chance to escalate into a more serious conflict. In other words, they simply function to smooth over tension that might build up between dogs resulting in a non-violent way of resolving a social conflict. Calming signals do not necessarily carry status significance. Clusters of calming signals should alert you to observe carefully. Adjustments to the environment, like increasing the space between dogs (or you and a dog), may be in order.

Displacement behavior

Most calming signals fall into a category of behavior which some people label as *displacement* activity. This is a behavior that seems irrelevant or out of place in a given situation, at least to humans. Say a dog has been asked to come, but she's conflicted about whether she wants to or not. So instead she does the zoomies—runs curving laps around the owner—or maybe she'll just sniff the ground. Humans do their own versions of this as well. You might know that you should mow the lawn before it rains, but instead you rearrange the living room furniture.

Here are some of the canine calming signals that Rugaas has identified as a result of her work.

SNIFFING

YAWNING

BLINKING

LICKING

TURNING AWAY

Some common calming signals.

Sniffing. Dogs use their noses to explore their environment, but excessive sniffing can be a calming signal. A dog who appears to be sniffing in a random manner is usually unsure about what is going on. It's a stalling tactic that can often be seen when an owner calls her dog to come, for example.

Yawning. Dogs yawn when things are getting tense. The dog may be holding his breath, and the deep inhalation and subsequent exhalation of a yawn acts to increase oxygen intake.

Blinking, averting eyes. Dogs approaching each other look away or make exaggerated eye blinks as a coping behavior. A human might gain the confidence of a worried dog more quickly by avoiding direct eye contact and turning away.

Stretching/flicking the tongue. A quick little flick forward of the dog's tongue often goes unnoticed because it is clouded by more obvious signals. It's another way for a dog to convey the same calming message. Both yawning and tongue flicking will often appear in photographs because dogs often find posing for a photo session to be stressful—trying to maintain a Sit-Stay during a face to face confrontation with a photographer who is likely a stranger. For dogs, it is intimidating being stared at by three eyes (two human, one a camera lens).

Curving and turning away. Curving is a form of greeting behavior. To avoid a head-to-head confrontation, a dog will often turn his eyes, head, or entire body away from another dog or person he finds somehow threatening. Curving and turning away may also show submission, the opposite of confrontational face-to-face, eye-to-eye contact. If the dog is somewhat unsure, his body will be stiff, and his tail held up stiff and high, perhaps wagging slowly as he curves or turns.

These dogs have approached each other by curving, avoiding a head-to-head confrontation.

Scratching. A dog who scratches himself, even though he doesn't have itchy skin, may be diffusing a potential conflict. This is often seen in situations where a little itch would be inconsequential, for example, in the face of a confrontation.

Splitting up. Some dogs take it upon themselves to split up two other dogs as they are interacting with each other. They will physically place themselves between the other dogs, most likely to help defuse potential conflicts. In my pet dog manners classes, our instructors use the principle of splitting by quietly stepping between two dogs who are staring at each other.

The play bow, what does it mean?

One interesting body language display you may see is the *play bow*. The bow, in which the dog places his front legs on the ground and raises his rear high in the air, seems to act as a social facilitator. It often serves as an invitation to play, and some think it may serve to make sure any playful growling or body postures are not taken in the wrong way. However, others consider a bow as evidence of the dog's inward state of confusion. The dog is ready to do something, but he is not sure what to do.

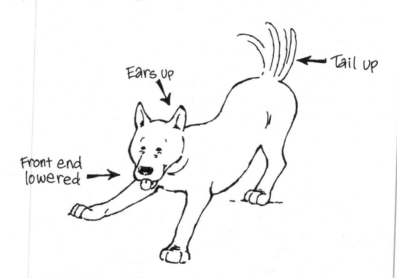

Fun almost always follows a play bow.

Stress behaviors

Stress results from whatever influence is at hand that changes a dog from his normal, neutral, state. It can make the dog more active than normal or less active than normal. It can be a happy state or an unhappy state. Stress is abstract and subjective. What's terribly stressful for one dog can be neutral or even enjoyable for another.

There's good stress and bad stress. Stress in manageable doses has a positive effect on dogs (and humans). It helps us perform to our potential. Human example: The final exam is in two days. I'd better quit messing around and study. That is "good" stress. However, too much stress inhibits the learning process because of chemical influences in the brain: The final exam is in an hour. I can't handle it, I'm just going to stay here in bed. That is "bad" stress.

Stressors leading to fear and anxiety behaviors activate the dog's *flight or fight* responses, contributing to behaviors such as problem barking or even biting. Stress hormones accumulate in the body and take a long time to dissipate. The effects of stress that may not become apparent until years later include immune system deficiencies, behavioral withdrawal, or a shortened life span.

Below is a list and illustrations of some of the common signs of stress. If you see clusters of two or more of these signs, pay attention. If you see even more, be thinking of how to manipulate the environment to make the dog more comfortable.

Panting. A dog who pants when not hot may be stressed. It can also be an indicator of physical problems. Or, maybe the dog just went for a run.

Drooling. Is it the anticipation of food, sexual arousal, or an upset stomach? Or is there something else in the dog's environment making him ill at ease?

Trembling. Again, we must look for clusters of signs, but shaking can be one indicator of stress. A dog might tremble from the cold, but if it's not cold out, a different stressor could be at work.

Sweaty paws. Why are there wet paw prints on the tile floor? It's not wet out. Consider stress. Dogs perspire through their paw pads.

Tense body. Sometimes you have to touch the dog to feel the rigidity. At other times, you can see tension just by the way the dog holds or moves his body.

Tense face. The dog might clench his jaws. The corners of the mouth could be drawn extremely forward or backward. The whisker beds might appear to be quivering due to tightening facial muscles. Extra wrinkles might appear about the muzzle.

Change in eyes. If your dog is wide-eyed, but it's not particularly dark out, the dilated pupils could be a sign of stress. The eyes of some very frightened dogs will show more white than normal. Some trainers call this "whale eye."

Personal space violations

Like people, dogs are concerned about their personal space, also known as "critical distance" or "flight zone." The size of such space varies depending on the situation, the personality of the dog, and how the dog was socialized. A dog's personal space may shrink when a familiar person approaches, i.e. he will let someone he knows and likes get close. But his personal space might expand if a stranger moves toward him. If the dog perceives someone or something is getting too close, he may react by freezing, flying (running away), or fighting. Many confrontations result from space issues. Much of canine communicative behavior is devoted to indicating tolerance (or lack of tolerance) at having others approach too closely.

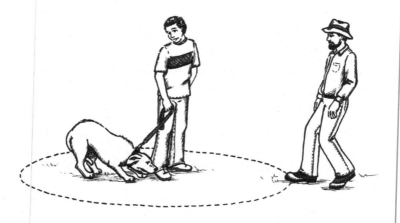

This dog's body language tells us that the stranger is beginning to invade his personal space.

This dog's body language tells us that he is not overly concerned about the approaching stranger.

The fight or flight responses are controlled by the brain's *limbic system*. By contrast, cognitive functions, such as learning and problem solving, are controlled by the brain's cerebral cortex. The limbic system integrates instinct with learning. If the limbic system is activated, the cerebral cortex is inhibited. Conversely, if the cerebral cortex is activated, the limbic system is inhibited. If a dog is trying to avoid a frightening or painful situation, whether real or imagined, the limbic system is engaged. He or she is unlikely to be able to "remember" previously learned cues like "Sit," "Stay," or "Come!" It's too late. The dog is on an irreversible instinctive path of self defense.

The 3 F's

Another way to categorize canine body language in relation to personal space threats are with the 3 F's:

1. **Freeze.** The dog is like a statue, staying perfectly still. A dog who freezes, frequently in a "small" or subordinate position, is likely afraid and stressed.

2. **Flight.** The dog, upon being approached, chooses to retreat, run, and/or hide from the cause of the worry.

3. **Fight.** The dog resorts to acting out, growling, lunging, snapping, or biting when the personal space violation pushes his stress tolerance beyond his ability to cope.

By the time you see one of the 3 F's, the dog is often already reactive to the point of being out of control. You need to watch for the more subtle signs that the dog is worried—such as calming signals or stress signals—before the dog adopts one of the 3 F's.

Here's a human example of invasion of personal space and how quickly the rules change according to the details of the situation. Imagine riding in an empty elevator. The doors open and a single person gets in and stands very close to you, shoulder touching your shoulder. You are uncomfortable about this situation. What if ten people got in and one person's shoulder was touching yours? The rules change. Personal space is dictated by many independent variables.

It may help if you think of your dog's critical space as imaginary circles of fluctuating size around the dog. Where the lines fall for these zones is not exact. The lines can change for the individual dog depending on factors such as environment, arousal level, the particular dog or person approaching, frontal or sideways approach, eye contact or lack of it, and overall stress threshold.

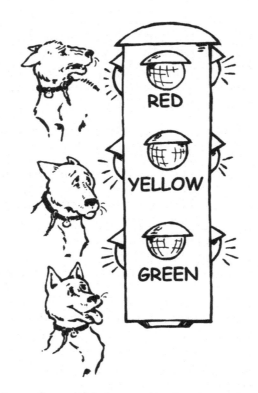

The three colors of a traffic signal light correspond to how dogs feel about their personal space at a particular point in time.

Green—Go. "It's safe, you can proceed. I'm not worried, I'm fine, it's a go, let's visit, I have no space problems." The body language will be relaxed or even excited. The dog may be straining to make contact. But be watchful, the dog may turn from green to yellow as an individual gets closer.

Yellow—Prepare to stop. "I'm a bit worried. I'm cautious. Please don't stress me further." This dog might show appeasement body language or offensively or defensively threatening behavior. The yellow light dog needs to feel secure that no one will enter his or her space uninvited.

Red—Stop. "Stop, don't come closer. I'm afraid or I'm angry." The defensive red light dog would rather leave or back up if given the option. Sometimes, due to obstacles like fences or short leashes, this is impossible and the dog will act out to keep the invader at bay. The offensive red light dog has no qualms about sending the invader off.

Once a dog is fully engaged with space issues (i.e., the light is red), he is on what I call the "slide of no return." Imagine yourself approaching a tall slide in a park. You have one foot on the lowest step of the ladder. There is time to change your mind and do something else. When you are at the top of the slide, you can still change your mind.

You can stay there or you can go back down the ladder. Once you are on your way down the slide, it's very difficult to stop or reverse the action.

Don't push your dog past the point of no return.

Your dog's physical well-being and its impact on behavior

A dog's physical condition can be a key to understanding his behavior and addressing a particular behavioral issue. As noted author, vet, and behaviorist Dr. Sophia Yin puts it:

> While behavioral problems in dogs are exceedingly common, sometimes behavioral signs are actually caused by or exacerbated by underlying medical issues. From the elderly housetrained Labrador Retriever who starts pottying in the house due to renal disease, diabetes or arthritis, to the Cocker Spaniel who suddenly snaps at family members due to pain and agitation from an ear infection, the first visit for sudden or persistent behavioral issues should be to your veterinarian.

Veterinary care is an often overlooked first course of action for training and behavior problems. A significant change in behavior can be one of the first signs of a currently invisible illness or physical problem. While not all veterinarians have a high level of expertise in behavioral issues, he or she can refer you to those that do. The good news is more and more vets are choosing to become certified in animal behavior and/or specialize in this field.

Visiting the vet

Ideally, routine wellness examinations should be performed by your vet twice a year. Puppies and senior dogs should be seen even more frequently. Because your dog ages at a faster rate than you, many subtle changes can develop over a six to twelve month period. Your vet can be an important resource in many matters. In addition to all of the illnesses that might plague your dog, a vet can probably also advise you on a number of other health issues that can impact behavior including:

- Nutrition.
- Spaying and neutering.
- Exercise.
- Dental care and grooming.

Your dog needs to see the vet regularly.

Optimum nutrition

Proper nutrition is fundamental to keeping all dogs healthy. Poor diet has been linked to all sorts of problems including behavior and training issues. Get help when evaluating commercially prepared food. If you are making your own dog food, be sure you first seek guidance from a veterinary professional. Recipes that sound good for your dog may not be so good for your dog. Do your homework. Remember to count your training treats as part of your dog's daily balanced diet.

Spaying and neutering

Spaying involves complete surgical removal of the uterus and ovaries. Often performed at about six months of age, some veterinarians will do the surgery or an alternative procedure earlier. Once spayed, females no longer go into heat. Thus, there will be no messy blood spotting around the house, no romantic males prowling your yard, and no unexpected pregnancies. One of the greatest benefits from spaying is a significant reduction (about 90%) in the chances of contracting breast cancer. Breast cancer is the leading form of cancer in females that haven't been spayed.

Since she is no longer subject to her biological urges, a spayed female is generally calmer and more responsive to her human family. She is less likely to roam in search of a mate or to get into fights, both of which can be dangerous and costly in terms of veterinary bills. And *you* get to avoid trying to confine her against her will.

Spaying, of course, prevents unwanted births. Unplanned pregnancies lead to unplanned expenses (such as extra feed bills, possible C-sections, and healthcare costs for the puppies), and disrupted routines (cleaning up after puppies, feeding puppies, finding homes for puppies, etc.).

Neutering the male involves complete surgical removal of the testicles. Routine neutering is a simple procedure causing only minimal discomfort. It is typically performed at about six months of age, but some veterinarians recommend doing the surgery or alternative procedures earlier.

There are many benefits of neutering. Male dogs are more likely to want to stay home and be content once they have been neutered, and they are apt to be less aggressive toward other dogs. Male dogs are more apt to develop the habit of urine marking than do females (lifting a leg on everything they encounter). Neutering helps control male urine marking. Other destructive behaviors are usually reduced because the dog is, in general, calmer. Neutered dogs also tend to be more responsive to their owners. They devote much less time and energy to proving themselves, defending territory, and breeding.

Routine exercise

Many dog owners underestimate the need for exercise. For many breeds of dogs, adequate exercise is a key to keeping physically and mentally healthy. It's amazing how many problem behaviors are improved by getting up a half hour earlier and walking the dog.

One of the benefits of exercise is that a tired dog is usually a well-behaved dog.

Dental care and grooming

If your dog looks matted, smells bad, or has bad breath, that's a dead give away that you've done too little in this department. Teeth especially tend to be neglected and lead quickly to abscesses, extractions, and related health problems. Professional cleanings may be necessary from time to time. Baths, brushing, nail trims—the program you follow depends on the individual. Get some recommendations from your network of dog professionals or your vet.

Use your vet as a resource for both health and behavioral issues.

Chapter 2

THE DRAWING BOARD

USING REWARDS

Make plans to use rewards as part of your training project.

When I was a little girl, our family used to listen to big band music. Here are some lyrics I remember from a song of that era:

> *Accentuate the positive, eliminate the negative,*
> *Latch on to the affirmative, get rid of Mr. In-between.*

It's great dog training advice! Let's put it into action. Humans are pretty good at catching their dogs doing something *wrong* and telling them off about it. But if you are honest and keep a careful eye on your dog, you'll probably find that he spends most of his day doing good stuff.

"Accentuate the positive"

A pretty simple concept you can use in your everyday life with your dog. See something you like? Tell your dog so by rewarding any appropriate behavior. Try to catch him in the act of doing something good.

"Eliminate the negative"

You get into a taxi in downtown Seattle. You tell the driver, "I don't want to go to the airport." You raise your voice, "Don't you dare take me to the Space Needle!" You begin gesturing wildly, "Driver, I don't want to go to the ferry terminal." You repeat, "I don't want to go to the ferry terminal." You again repeat, *"No,* I told you I don't want to go to the ferry terminal!" At this point, the taxi driver will likely become frustrated with the lack of helpful information. It is the same with your dog.

The biology of rewards

Biologists can divide natural canine behavior motivation into three basic categories: (1) food acquisition, (2) hazard avoidance, and (3) reproduction. As you will see, my program utilizes food acquisition sequences, including play, as rewards.

Rewards drive behavior

You've heard of the Law of Gravity. Well, we dog trainers talk about the Law of Effect. The Law of Effect is just about as predictable as the Law of Gravity. Paraphrased, part of the Law of Effect reads: "If a behavior is followed by a satisfying result, that behavior is apt to become stronger." Many of you recognize this concept as *positive reinforcement.* Positive means to add something, reinforcement means something that makes the behavior stronger.

Here are some examples of behaviors—some we like, some we don't—that can be strengthened in one way or another through positive reinforcement.

- A dog looks out a window and enjoys seeing a bird fly by. She's more apt to look out that window again, in the hope of seeing another bird. The looking-out-the-window-behavior has been rewarded, hence strengthened.

- Granny approaches and the dog happens to remain sitting on the floor instead of jumping up. Granny gives him a treat—the dog is more likely to sit the next time Granny approaches. The sit-when-someone-approaches has been rewarded, hence strengthened.

- A dog whines and is happy to discover that her owner immediately gets up and takes her for a walk. She will likely whine again, perhaps louder and longer next time. A behavior the owner does not like, whining-for-attention, has been rewarded, hence strengthened.

Here is a common situation. The dog is rewarded for begging, and the begging behavior is strengthened.

Just what is a reinforcer for your dog?

Anything that makes a behavior stronger is termed a *reinforcer*. (I will use the words "reinforcer" and "reward" interchangeably.) Many dog trainers usually use food as a reinforcer, but toys and social interactions can be rewards for dogs, too. Strength of behavior can be measured in any number of ways including, but not limited to, the frequency, intensity, or duration of the behavior.

The rewards that you provide your dog for good behavior work to make *you* more interesting from the dog's perspective. If you are the source of good things, your dog will want to keep paying attention to you—and that is a very good thing. Until you build a training relationship with your dog in which he views you as a key to earning rewards, you are competing with lots of environmental distractions. Let your dog know that you can trump the leaf fluttering by or the sound of someone else opening the refrigerator door. He'll play the attention lottery and ask himself, "Which is apt to pay off?" This book helps you stack the deck in your favor. *Learning how to focus your dog's attention on you is a foundation stone in training.* All buildings need a firm foundation or they are apt to collapse later, no matter how good they look at first glance. The same is true with dog training.

Reward charts

Let's start by doing some planning. You intend to train your dog—let's call him Gus—to be the perfect pet. First, figure out the best rewards for him by filling out the chart below. Gus will tell you what to put into the blanks if you pay close attention to him. Conduct some "market research" with Gus to discover a few high ranking items for each of the columns—food, toys, and interactions. Work with Gus to determine which items he's most attracted to. You might choose a bright red plastic ball. Given a choice, however, you might find that Gus would rather work for a plain old slimy tennis ball. A good reinforcement item will catch and maintain your dog's interest even if other exciting things are going on around him.

Reward chart for your dog

	FOOD	TOYS	INTERACTIONS
1			
2			
3			
4			
5			

Keep working with Gus until you have five foods, five toys, and five interactions that really capture his attention. Don't worry if you have trouble deciding what reward goes into what category. The important thing is that you end up with fifteen different rewards. To help get you started, here is a reward chart for a typical dog.

	FOOD	TOYS	INTERACTIONS
1	Cheese	Food stuffed toy	Go for a walk
2	Bits of turkey franks	Squeaker toy	Playing fetch
3	Liver treats	Rope toy	Ride in the car
4	Chicken white meat	Fleece toy	Being petted, praised
5	Regular kibble	Rubber bone	Tug of war

The use of food as a reward

For the vast majority of dogs, the reward of choice is food. It's a *primary* reinforcer. Survival instincts dictate most dogs will be highly receptive to activities associated with the acquisition of food. Even though pet dogs no longer need to figure out how to find and catch their own dinner, they are still genetically programmed to be alert and responsive when food is available—you might see that in your own dog whenever you head into the kitchen. Let's take advantage of it.

Rather than have food in a bowl down at all times, feed Gus scheduled meals. It will help you in your training to know when Gus is hungry. One strategy is to save some (or all!) of your dog's normal daily allotment of food for use in training exercises. Your dog might react well to extra special treats while in training, but make sure they count as part of your dog's daily balanced diet.

There are a wide variety of commercially prepared treats on the market. Take the time to read the label and consider the ingredients completely. Note that some dogs have allergies to food such as peanuts or wheat. If you are using a commercially-prepared kibble as a training treat, you can make it more attractive by shaking it up in a plastic bag with a piece of cheese or liver. Small pieces of soft food don't need chewing and are less apt to crumble, fall to the floor, or distract your dog from the task at hand. You can make treats last twice as long by cutting the pieces in half.

Ideas for home-made treats
Low fat cheese cut into 1/8 inch cubes. If the cheese comes in stick or string form, simply slice off little circles, or keep the whole stick in your pouch or hand and pinch it off as needed. Slice **turkey franks** into thin coins, microwave until firm, or keep it whole and pinch off as needed. Dogs learn to take little dabs of **squeeze cheese** right from the nozzle. Refrigerate all perishable foods.

Treat delivery
How you deliver treats will vary depending on the training exercise. Usually it will work best to feed your dog directly from your hand. Try feeding him only very small pieces of food. That way he always has to make contact with your fingers which further strengthens the notion that you are the source of this wonderful treat. But what if Gus is a little rough when taking food from your hand? If so, don't take your hand away, simply keep it there and hold on tighter to the piece of food. Don't scold or threaten him, just wait until he becomes gentler and then release the food to him. If Gus barks or paws at your hand, remain calm and slowly turn away. Slowly (don't snatch it away quickly or you might encourage Gus to be grabby) put the food back in your pouch, pocket, or hold it to your stomach until he settles down. If he's too focused and single-minded about the food, do your training exercises after his meal when he's calmer, or change to a lower ranking food treat from your reward chart.

For overly ambitious dogs or for people with tender fingers, here's an alternative plan: Place the tidbit into the bowl of a metal teaspoon. Direct the handle of the spoon along your wrist so that only the hollow of the spoon and food are in your fingers. Put your thumb over the food. Now if the dog bites too hard, contact will be made with the metal, which is not very pleasant. Take your thumb off the food when your dog's lips become gentle. You do not need to say a thing. Gus will learn to accept food nicely.

Use the spoon technique to teach your dog to accept food gently.

Most of the time, feeding directly from your hand is the way to go. But for some behaviors, it may work better to toss a treat directly to Gus (when teaching him to Stay,
for example) while other times it will work better to throw the treat a few feet to move
Gus away from you. This subject will be covered later in the book.

The use of toys and games as rewards

Playing with toys and engaging in games could be thought of as a relic of food acquisition behavior. Your dog may approach a toy much like he would a prey animal. In
the wild, a predator listens, looks, sniffs, and orients toward the prey. Next comes the
stalk, run, grab, and hold. Depending on the size of the prey there is a shake or bringing down of the prey, the kill, and perhaps dismemberment. You might think about
this when you see your dog chasing and catching a flying disc, playing with a tug toy,
chewing up a stick, or peeling the skin off a tennis ball. How many of us know a dog
whose aim in life is to take the squeak out of squeaky toys?

You filled out a rewards chart for Gus which listed some toys that are to be kept for
training. Put them away after use to keep them "fresh" and special. I like toys small
enough that they can be hidden in my hand or pocket. Squeaky balls that collapse
work well. Small, furry, squeaky creatures with eyes are also intriguing to some dogs.
They are easily hidden in your pocket or on a window sill to be brought out as a
surprise game to reward a training exercise. Be sure these toys are large enough so
that your dog doesn't swallow them by accident. Toys with a tail or handle are a safer
choice, easier to work with and can still be stuffed up your sleeve. A leash made of a
tug rope material is also handy. You can drop the handle to the dog and have some tug
fun. You can keep the dog guessing as to when his leash will turn into an interactive
toy.

Certain toys your dog finds rewarding should be reserved for training. Put them away between training sessions.

Which is the better reinforcement, food or toys?

It depends. Toys are especially appropriate as rewards for active exercises like Come. A bit of food might help steady a stationary exercise like Down. Use of toys is more time-consuming than use of small food rewards. The food is gobbled and gone—then the dog is all ready for what happens next. With a toy, you eventually have to get it back. Taking it away could be a disappointment for Gus. Remember, the ultimate purpose of the toy is to make *you* more interesting and rewarding. Once he learns how charming and interesting you are, you won't always have to rely on bottomless pockets full of toys and food to maintain his attention.

Different toys for different dogs

Like people, dogs have different preferences in toys and games. You like to play cards, your sister might prefer playing tennis. My dog likes squeaky toys, your dog might prefer a fleecy tug toy. Experiment—your dog has the answers. You may need to put effort into animating the toy. Hide it in your pocket, bring it out suddenly. Throw it up in the air, pretend it's getting away. Talk to the toy. You'll get your dog's attention and maybe the neighbors', too! We call these "toys," but they are effective tools to help you build a great pet.

Balls for ball crazy dogs. A ball crazy dog will usually be happy with any old ball. For your comfort, however, a ball on a rope provides a less slippery handle, making it easier to take the ball from the dog's mouth. It doesn't roll as far when thrown, increasing your control over both the ball and dog. The way it flutters as it flies through the air and rolls on the ground will excite most dogs. Make your own by knotting a ball into the toe of an old sock.

Transformer toys for uninterested dogs. There are some dogs who haven't learned to enjoy playing with toys. The good thing, however, is that few dogs need encouragement to take a food treat. So, a solution for an "uninterested dog" is to transform a toy into a vessel to provide food. There are toys on the market with Velcro pockets designed so you can open the toy to replace a broken squeaker. They must have been designed by a dog savvy person! Just pull it open and insert a high value treat. This game is a cooperative effort. Play with your dog, but when the game is over, *you* are the one to open the pocket and give your dog the food. Then, put the toy away for next time.

Reluctance to give up the toy. One downside of using toys as reinforcers is that some dogs do not want to give them back! Many dogs are just that way, especially when it comes to tug-of-war toys. Be happy you have identified such a high value reinforcement! Brute strength and outrunning your dog won't work. Plan "trade training" sessions separately from playing sessions. It will be easier to teach the "trading" concept when Gus is not already excited from playing the game.

Your dog loves the toy, but how do you get it back?

The trade method. Start with a pouch of goodies and a low-ranking, somewhat boring toy. Choose a toy with a handle that allows you a good grip. Keep Gus on a leash so he can't play keep away. When Gus has the toy in his mouth, bring out a treat. Show it to him. If all goes well, he'll open his mouth for the treat and you take the toy. Yes, it's a bribe, but you are getting Gus to practice giving up a toy! It's a start. As soon as your dog swallows the food, give the toy back. Hmm, he gets a treat and the toy! Good deal for Gus! To up the ante, you might even give him a better toy that you have hidden ahead of time in your pocket!

You don't need to say anything at this point, just work on willing exchanges. We want to make sure he understands and trades politely before you add a cue, like the word "Give." It's better for him not to hear "Give" at all until you know he's had enough practice to release the toy willingly and happily. Three to five training sessions a day, with only three to five trade repetitions in each session should give you and Gus a good foundation of willing exchanges.

Use the trade method to convince your dog to give up a toy.

Training lingo: sessions and reps

The time of day that you set aside to train is referred to as a *session.* Dogs learn better if you train in several short sessions than one or two relatively long sessions. *Reps* are the number of times you repeat an exercise during a session. As with sessions, don't overdo it with too many reps. The idea is to quit while the dog is still having fun and is motivated to participate. As a general rule, I usually recommend three to five sessions per day, and three to five reps per session. That means anywhere from nine to 25 reps for each exercise each day.

The dead tug toy method. Tug toys aren't fun when they don't tug back. If Gus becomes overly stimulated or won't release the toy when asked, stop playing, be quiet, and plant your feet. Slowly, hand over hand, work up the handle of the toy until you are holding it right against his mouth. Now the dog's nose is against your hands and your hands are tight against your body. Very little tug action can take place. Not much fun. Wait patiently and don't react. Gus might continue tugging while you hold. He might even tug harder. Just be quiet, don't even look at Gus, just wait. Sooner or later he will become bored and eventually let go. When he does so, immediately jump into action, be fun and offer the game of tug again. Your dog will learn when you "stall out" he can jump start you by releasing the toy. He thinks he's training you to start playing again. You know you are training him to give up the toy. Both of you are happy. Vary the number of repetitions you do in a session to keep Gus guessing as to when you plan to end the session and put the toy away.

Social interactions as rewards

In the third column of the rewards chart on page 28 you listed five interactions. There are many every day activities you do together that don't involve food or toys, but are still very rewarding for your dog. Some are powerful—like going for a car ride or going for a walk. Some are simple—a quick tummy rub or words of praise. Whatever interaction you choose, plan ahead and set it up so that sometimes these rewards can immediately follow a successful training exercise. This could be done by having the leash or car keys readily available. Bringing the leash or car keys into view can have an immediate impact and will bridge the gap of getting to the door with Gus for the walk or ride. Don't lie to your dog. If you get the leash, *do* go for a walk, even a brief one. If you grab the keys, *do* let him jump into the car. You need only go around the block.

More important points concerning reinforcement

Here's a quick introduction to two concepts that will be used throughout the book. Modern dog trainers use two different categories or schedules of reinforcement: *Continuous* and *intermittent.* You'll have both in your toolbox.

Continuous schedule of reinforcement

A continuous schedule of reinforcement works best when you are teaching your dog a new behavior. When starting out on something new, the dog should be reinforced for every correct response, i.e., continuously. You will notice that throughout this book, when introducing a new behavior, I will recommend you use a very high rate of reinforcement by rewarding every response that the dog gets right (dog trainers call getting it right *meeting your criteria*). Continuous reinforcement will help a dog learn with minimal frustration and maximum attention as he tries to master something new. In order to be successful at this and keep your dog "in the game" a judgm,nt call has to be made as you train: The criteria needs to be low enough for the dog to be successful at earning that high rate of reinforcement. For the exercises in this book, a rule of thumb is to keep the exercise easy enough that Gus can get it right at least ten times in one minute. Selection of appropriate criteria and rate of reinforcement is a juggling act you will become more comfortable with as you gain experience.

Intermittent schedule of reinforcement

An intermittent schedule of reinforcement works best to sustain a behavior that your dog has already begun to master. Once your dog has learned the behavior, there will be times when I recommend that a "correct" behavior not be rewarded. In fact, you might not reward your dog until he does the behavior correctly several times in a row. I call these "two-fers" or "three-fers," meaning the dog must get the behavior right two or three times (and so on) to earn a reward. In other words, you are going to vary the ratio of reinforcements, 2:1 or 3:1, rather than 1:1. This should do away with any fear you might have that the dog won't perform unless you have food in your pocket. You will be taught how to vary the rewards later in the book when we begin actual training exercises.

Chapter 3

Building Supplies

Some Useful Equipment

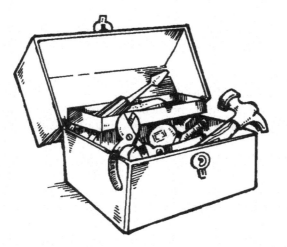

You should have a good assortment of tools to help train and care for your family dog.

In addition to a supply of carefully selected rewards, your toolbox should include a variety of dog training and care equipment. In this chapter, I will briefly review the equipment you need and some of the benefits they provide. More detailed use of these items as training tools will be covered in the following chapters.

- Toys.
- Collars.
- Leashes.
- Harnesses.

- Plastic Poop Bags.
- Mats/Beds.
- Crates.
- Clickers.
- Treat pouches.

Toys

As mentioned earlier, some toys should be dedicated for training rewards only, to be put away until the next time you have a training session. However, dogs should also have free access to other toys. Young or high energy dogs really appreciate having some free access toys lying around to play with whenever they want—especially chew toys. It's comforting for you to know that if Gus feels like chewing, he has options other than your furniture. I recommend that you rotate these free access toys. Keep most of them in a closet, but every few days rotate few "new" toys out for the dog. Put the "old" toys back in the closet for a rest.

Allow Gus to try out all toys thoroughly before leaving some of them down when no one is home. If it appears the toy can break, or might be small enough to get lodged in his mouth or cause frustration, get rid of it and try a different toy.

Hollow rubber toys

Premier Pet Products and the Kong Company both have interesting hollow rubber shaped toys that entertain by bouncing and rolling erratically when nudged or dropped. Purchase a size large enough that it cannot be swallowed by your dog.

These toys with hollowed out spaces can also be stuffed with a portion of your dog's dinner, providing a pleasant pastime for an underemployed dog. Mixing in a little bit of canned food will keep dry kibble from falling out too quickly. So will a wad of bread. Be creative by layering special treats like a tiny piece of cheese or bit of meat with the kibble. Make a hot weather pacifier by sealing off one end with peanut butter and filling it with water. Add a pinch of bullion powder and shake well. Stand it on end in a cup and freeze. Rinse the "pup-sicle" with warm water before serving to get the frost off.

Rubber toys that can be stuffed with food are a great way to keep your dog occupied.

You might consider providing several stuffed toys! I know dogs that eat their entire breakfast out of them! Keep the toys clean, especially in hot weather or where insects are prevalent. They do well on the top rack of the dishwasher! I put mine in the clothes washer with hot water and soap. It's a bit noisy, but gets the job done in no time.

Hollow chew bones
Commercially processed natural hollow bones from a pet shop may be safer than real bones from your butcher. Butcher bones can splinter and cause health problems. Some bones come pre-stuffed with goodies, or you can do it yourself.

Kibble dispensing toys
Your little predator can forage indoors with the best thing since the Pez candy dispenser—kibble dispensing toys for dogs! They come in a variety of interesting sizes and shapes produced by several different manufacturers. The openings in the toys can be adjusted so that the rate they give up the food varies. Dogs nose it, paw it, scoot it across the floor and keep busy gobbling up the food as it falls out.

The more your dog pushes or rolls the toy around, the more treats he can earn.

More than one dog sharing toys?

Dogs can get into arguments over toys. Think this over carefully, especially before leaving more than one dog home alone together with a prized possession.

Collars, harnesses, leashes

In days gone by, the term "choke chain" was synonymous with obedience training. Now, most dog trainers are going by the motto "Use brains, not chains" meaning there are alternative ways to train dogs which don't rely on brute strength, intimidation, or pain.

Your dog's collar or harness should include identification information. Your last name and phone number or email address can help get you and your dog back together should he become lost. I also recommend that you ask your veterinarian about microchips or tattoos as a means of permanent identification. If you are shopping for collars, harnesses, or leashes, here are some points to consider before you buy.

Buckle collars

Regular buckle collars are fine, but correct fit is critical. Dogs with narrow heads and small ears, such as Greyhounds or Dobermans, are more at risk for backing out of collars, especially new, stiff collars. Find the right balance between being snug enough so the dog can't back up and pull out of it, and loose enough to be comfortable. A new leather collar can be made softer by rubbing it with shaving cream or shoe conditioner.

Premier collars

Another good alternative is a collar which tightens slightly when tension is placed on it, preventing a dog from pulling free. Premier is a brand name for collars known generically as half checks or martingales. They're much safer than the traditional choke collar because they cannot constrict any further than the safety loop. When the collar is new and stiff, the smaller loop might not lie down flat. To make the collar softer, run it through the washing machine, stretch it flat, and let it air dry.

A martingale collar provides a bit more security than a traditional buckle collar.

The trouble with collars

Almost any collar can accidentally get caught on something, presenting a serious problem to an unsupervised dog. Cases could be built for both wearing and not wearing collars. The decision is yours.

Gentle Leader head collar

Each brand of head collar is designed differently. The technique for their use is different too. My head collar of choice is the Gentle Leader which I have used in my training school for more than twenty years. I find the Gentle Leader especially helpful for dogs who like to pull. It's similar to a halter on a horse—where the head goes, the animal will follow. Like a halter, the Gentle Leader does not put pressure on the dog's tender throat; it fits up higher and rests on the jawbones. The strap around the muzzle delivers an additional message of control. Follow directions on fit and use carefully. These head collars were designed to be used on a very short leash without jerking or constant pressure by the owner. It should be used in conjunction with positive reinforcement.

The Gentle Leader collar is my choice for dogs who like to pull.

Choke, pinch, or shock collars
None of these three are needed in reward-based training. While some dogs who are relatively immune to pain appear to learn very quickly on pain producing collars due to the surprise effect, the negatives outweigh the benefits for most dogs. Read more about compulsive training and it's fall-out in Chapter 8.

Regular harnesses
Conventional harnesses are okay for every day wear and for training. Due to health issues, some dogs cannot tolerate a collar and might be more comfortable in a harness. The only drawback is that some dogs feel compelled to pull against the opposition of a harness, but training can change that.

Easy Walk harnesses
With an Easy Walk harness, the leash is attached to a ring on the *front* chest strap. When fitted properly, the front attachment harness encourages dogs to stay in balance instead of pulling, allowing the leash to be slack and both of you to enjoy your walk.

Regular leashes
For versatility, choose a leash between four and six feet long, made of leather or fabric. It's about right to go for an informal walk, and for training, too. It's long enough to allow you some distance from your dog when you are practicing stays, but not so bulky that it can't be gathered in your hands for close work.

Retractable leashes
A spring-loaded retractable leash is okay for informal walks. I consider them too awkward for training exercises. Retractable leashes tend to teach some dogs to pull—be-

cause they are rewarded for doing so by getting further ahead. Should you accidentally drop it, the plastic handle becomes a missile aimed directly at your dog. The round thin cord can be hazardous if it tangles around you and your dog and exasperating when it gets caught up on bushes. An alternative is a long line which is either a fabric or leather leash between ten and 30 feet in length.

Leashes can work against you—literally!
The dog's opposition reflex makes a dog pull against pressure. Try it out. Slip your finger into Gus's collar and pull slightly. Does your dog move away from or into the pressure? Unless overpowered or successfully trained otherwise, dogs instinctively oppose force. This is one of the main reasons a pulling dog keeps on pulling.

Plastic poop bags
Ethically and legally, you need to clean up if your dog defecates on property other than your own. Handy little rolls of perfectly sized bags are available in a variety of colors at pet shops. You will probably also want to have a long handled pooper scooper for use at home.

Beds and rugs
If your dog has a comfy bed to call his own, he's less apt to hang around on your bed or furniture. Training your dog to go to a designated rug when the doorbell rings or during family dinners—as a means of control—is covered in Chapter 6.

Crates
Crates are small kennels made of wire, plastic, or nylon. They are convenient safety measures when riding in an auto. Crates are also helpful in supervision during the various aspects of housetraining. Details on the appropriate use of crates are found in the Chapter 4 on Relationship Building and in the Housetraining section of Chapter 5.

Clickers
Should you decide to use a clicker when training your dog (see The Mark of Distinction in Chapter 4 for more information) you will have a wide variety of choices. The most common are square box type clickers with a metal panel inserted for your thumb to activate. Some of the newer models have raised buttons that are more easily operated. A clicker makes a sharp, crisp sound that helps you communicate to your dog that he has done something you want to reinforce. Since some dogs are somewhat sound-sensitive, you can find clickers that are quieter than most of the ones on the market. There are even electronic markers made especially for dog trainers.

Clickers come in a variety of styles, but this is the most common type.

Treat pouches

As mentioned in Chapter 2, a treat pouch provides you a way to have quick and easy access to treats while training. Timely delivery of treats is critical in dog training. I recommend a pouch to keep your treats accessible and organized. While there are many brands available on the market, I particularly like the Premier Treat Pouch. It attaches to your waist with a belt and has a hinged opening that allows it to stay wide open, but can be snapped shut securely with a nudge of your elbow.

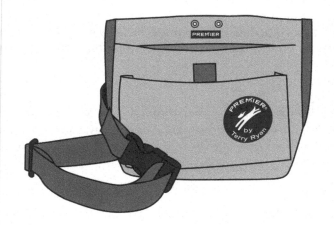

A treat pouch allows you quick and easy access to rewards for your dog.

Chapter 4

THE FOUNDATION

A RELATIONSHIP BUILDING PROGRAM

A good foundation allows you to start building a solid framework for your relationship with your dog.

Much has been written about the human-animal bond and the benefits experienced by both people and dogs who share their lives with one another. An appropriate relationship and effective communication channels are the foundation blocks needed for living successfully with a dog. My definition of an appropriate relationship is mutual trust, plus cooperation without domination. You are your dog's life-long guidance counselor.

Here are some life-skill exercises that will give you a firm head start foundation upon which you can build future training:

- **The "Mark of Distinction."**
- **Catch Him in the Act of Doing Something Good.**
- **You Called?**
- **The Off Switch.**
- **Gotcha.**
- **Let's Go (but please don't pull).**
- **Helping the Latchkey Dog.**
- **The Boomerang Come.**

The "Mark of Distinction"

Goal: Establish clear communication channels enabling your dog to receive information in black and white, not shades of gray. English is, at best, a very weak second language for Gus. Influence the behavior of your dog not by words, but by your actions.

The term "clicker training" is applied to the concept of using a *marker* followed by delivery of a reward. "Mark" or "marker" is an informal term for the sound a trainer uses to pinpoint a particular bit of behavior—hence the phrase "the Mark of Distinction." It communicates, "This is what I want and now I'm gonna reward you for doing it!"

Using a marker and a reward is very effective for teaching your dog new behaviors.

A variety of markers can be used

Most trainers use the sound of a click produced by a small hand-held device called a clicker as their marker and food as a reward. Most dogs respond well to the sound of clickers and their use is gaining popularity all over the world. Some trainers make a clicking sound with their mouths rather than holding a clicker. Other trainers use a verbal marker by saying a simple, but novel word, like "Yes" or the word "Click." The benefit of a word is that you can't misplace it and it leaves both of your hands free for other aspects of training, like delivering a treat and holding on to the leash! A verbal marker needs to be short, snappy, and salient. The sound should be novel enough to stand out. The word "Good!" for example makes a poor marker. It is short and snappy, but not novel since you probably tell Gus he's a good boy numerous times throughout the day. It's better to start with something new and carefully build the meaning into the word.

Markers are not just for dogs

You might have noticed whistles around the necks of marine mammal trainers. They use a tweet of the whistle as their marker and then deliver a fish. TAG (Teaching with Acoustical Guidance) is an effective way of using a marker for human-to-human communication as well.

Practice your timing without your dog

Before you actually start to use your marker and food to train Gus, please practice the timing of the use of the marker all by yourself. While you practice, put Gus away until you get good at this! These first few exercises are just for you.

Drop a set of keys. See if you can time the sound of your marker to the sound of the keys hitting the floor. Whether saying a word or using a clicker, practice keeping your body still so that your marker is not overshadowed by your actions! Drop a tennis ball. Try to time your marker to coincide with the sound of the bounce. Be ready! It will bounce again! Try to match every bounce until the ball quits bouncing and rolls away! Ask a friend to walk across the floor at varying speeds. Mark every time your friend's left heel makes contact with the floor. Not the whole sole of the shoe, not the toe, not the right foot, but only the heel of the left foot. This will help with your eye-hand coordination. Ask your friend to keep an eye on you. If you clicked and thrust your clicker hand forward at the same time, which will your dog pick up on as a marker? The sound? The arm movement? Will he be conditioned to both at one time? Don't muddy it up with extra words of praise. Keep it simple by keeping still, quiet, and letting the marker and food do the communicating. You can cuddle and praise your dog later.

When you become consistent at marking the defined *criteria* (i.e., the object hitting the floor in the examples above), practice delivering food—no dog yet! Save an empty toilet paper tube and place it on a table in front of you. This represents your dog's mouth. Have your supply of food bits in your pocket or in your treat pouch.

Now do three to five repetitions of this sequence:

- Keep your entire body still, then sound the marker.
- After the marker sound, reach for and deliver a food treat to the tube.

You want the marker to precede the delivery of the food, not occur simultaneously with it. Practice this several times a day. Did you knock the tube over? You will get better with practice. Keep repeating the exercise until you become comfortable with the mark and feed sequence.

Be a splitter, not a lumper

Two of my mentors, Marian Breland-Bailey and Bob Bailey, taught me to "be a splitter, not a lumper." Break a task into easy little pieces. This increases the chance for success. Success is what earns Gus a mark and treat. The rate of reinforcement goes up. Rewards drive behavior!

Bring out the dog

The first training exercise that involves Gus will take place only once, involving a quick series of three to five sessions of three to five repetitions each. Then, you will be ready to move on. This is called "charging the marker." It's an example of *classical conditioning,* where the dog learns to associate two events—in this case, a particular sound with food.

Keeping in mind the timing exercises you have learned without Gus, sound your marker and immediately give him a piece of food. Once you have completed the three to five sessions, you are done and ready to move on to marking actual behaviors.

With this exercise, you are not training your dog to *do* anything in particular. This is just a brief introductory learning experience to help him understand that the sound of the marker means food is on the way. Gus can be doing any neutral, acceptable, or good behavior as you sound the marker and feed. It's a good idea not to mark and feed during an unacceptable behavior such as barking, jumping on you, or mouthing your hand—you wouldn't want to inadvertently reinforce for an inappropriate behavior! Gus will "get it" in just a few sessions and will remember the meaning of the marker. You two are now ready to mark and feed "real" behaviors!

The mark is a promise
Don't break a promise. If you accidentally mark at the wrong time—give a treat. There is always a next time. Don't devalue your marker by not rewarding. You now have an important communication tool that can be used to teach new behaviors.

"Catch Him in the Act of Doing Something Good"
Goal: Reinforce random acts of goodness. You will be using your marker and bits of food for this exercise also. "Catch Him in the Act of Doing Something Good" is formally known as *"capturing a behavior."* Capturing a behavior is one of many methods you will learn about in this book to get a desired behavior from Gus.

Keep in mind that for this exercise we are:

- No longer charging the marker. That was a one-time exercise and has been accomplished.

- Not trying to make a behavior happen. We are waiting for it to happen by itself.

- Not using a verbal cue for the behavior. All of that comes later.

What we *are* practicing is paying more attention to Gus and focusing on "catching," via the mark and feed technique, a spontaneous behavior that we want him to repeat.

Here are some real life practical examples of Gus unexpectedly doing something "right" that you might want to reinforce. The first three are just for fun, the last three have real practical applications.

"What was that?" It's darling when Gus cocks his head to one side. You probably know what the precursors are for his head cock. Does he "get that look in his eye?"

Does he stop breathing for a second? Watch for it! Be ready to catch the head cock with a mark and feed.

"Take a bow." Big spontaneous stretches with the rear up and elbows on the ground are fun to capture. Wait until his elbows are actually on the ground before you mark. After having captured this behavior, you can eventually train Gus to "Take a bow," a great way to warm up your dog before a walk!

"You're all wet!" The big shake off that dogs do when they want to relax or want to get rid of water on their fur could be captured. They often do it when they get up from a nap. Wait until Gus is totally into his shake off, then mark and feed.

You can use the Mark of Distinction to catch and reinforce a fun behavior like this.

Gus goes to his rug. Company has arrived with the usual excitement associated with greetings. This time you notice that Gus quit mugging your guest and calmed down more quickly than usual and went to his rug to lie down. Mark his getting on the rug and go over and deliver a treat to him. It might be less than polite to your guest, but it's great dog training!

Gus sits at the door. You and Gus are ready to go for a walk. The leash is on and you approach the door. He happens to sit by the door this time. Mark and feed that spontaneous sit. If he doesn't sit, no problem. Just go out the door and see if he sits the next time.

Gus has learned that if he sits after you put his leash on he will be rewarded.

Gus stops at a boundary. Gus is not supposed to go into the dining room because of the brand new hardwood floors you have just installed. Most of the time he "forgets" while he is following you around the house, and just steps in. This time you enter the dining room and notices that he stopped, all by himself, at the threshold. Capture and reward that behavior!

Later, in Chapters 6 and 7, we'll talk about how to get these behaviors without waiting for them to happen, how to make them reliable, and how to put them on a verbal cue to show off to your friends. For now, just remember: See the behavior, mark the behavior, and give the food.

Keep practicing your mechanical skills

Get a pair of dice. Decide ahead of time if you are going to respond to "odd" numbers or "even" numbers. Let's say you are "even." Throw the dice on a table. See how fast you can do the math and decide if it's odd or even. If it's even, sound your marker! Pick up and roll again. If it's odd, do not mark, just pick the dice up and roll again. Repeat.

Variation for two people: Your friend responds only to odd numbers. Throw the dice. If an odd number results, your friend has to mark as soon as possible, pick up the dice, and roll again. Is it an even number this time? You are responding only to even numbers, so you mark, grab the dice, and roll again. Whoever marks, odd or even, also picks up and rolls the dice for the next turn.

Dice game taught to me by Japanese clicker trainer Kazuya Arai.

"You Called?"

Goal: In spite of distractions, Gus happily focuses on you when you call his name. Some people use their dog's name indiscriminately. For example, they expect the dog to come when they call his name. Next, they expect the dog to get out of the trash by saying his name in a threatening way. Refrain from putting a bad "spin" on your dog's name. I know this sounds radical, but if you've poisoned your dog's name ("Gus, Bad! Stop it, Gus!"), consider giving him a new one so you don't have to unload the bad association baggage before you establish his name as an attention getter and precursor to all good things.

If you yell "Gus, No!" every time you are angry with your dog, you can poison his name.

For this exercise, you will use a toy and your own charm. No food. No marker. Your challenge? Making yourself fun for your dog. Select a toy Gus likes a lot—maybe his squeaky mouse. This should be one of those special training toys we talked about that don't end up on the floor with the rest of his free access toys.

Here's the plan: Keep the toy in a secure spot. Three to five times a day, pull the toy out and get Gus's attention with it. Move it from side to side, hide it in your pocket, and then make it pop out again while acting surprised. Talk to the toy, then throw it up and catch it. Pretend it's running away, but grab it at the last moment. Gus will wonder what's going on. When he's clearly paying attention to all the fun you are having without him, happily call his name *once,* and immediately engage him in play for at least three seconds with the toy. Help Gus give it up politely and put it in your pocket until the next time.

The "You Called?" exercise helps Gus learn that when he hears his name it means "Pay attention, something great is going to happen." The trick is to be sure something great does happen! After playing with him a few seconds, feel free to immediately add other fun stuff like pats, praise, or jumping into the car to go for a ride. To avoid confusion with future exercises, please do not use food rewards for this attention game. In this case, you are practicing using *yourself* as a primary reinforcer. Just be charming and fun for your dog. Put the toy away when you're done. Hide the toy in different locations. A drawer, your pocket, in the refrigerator! Call your dog's name and suddenly make the toy appear for a game. Wow! Aren't you interesting! Gus had better keep an eye on you. You can make toys appear from anywhere.

There will be times in the future when you may desperately need Gus's attention. By doing these positive exercises now, you are putting money into the "pay attention to me account" so that you'll have plenty to draw on in a time of emergency.

"Off Switch"
Goal: Lower the excitement level in your dog.

As you begin to use rewards in your training, your dog may often get excited. The "Off Switch" exercise will help your dog settle down when necessary and be rewarded for calm behavior. For this exercise, you won't be using the marker or food or even a toy. You will be using social interaction as the reward.

It doesn't matter if you or the dog is standing, sitting, or lying down. Put the fingers of one hand over Gus's thigh or shoulder muscle. Lightly push his skin over the muscle in a slow little circle. Then pick up your hand, put it on another muscle, and push that area of skin in a little circle. The circular movement should be as slow as possible. Your fingers stay in the same place on the same bit of skin so there is no friction between fingers and fur. The hand moves the skin over the muscle. Think pleasant thoughts. Breathe slowly and deeply.

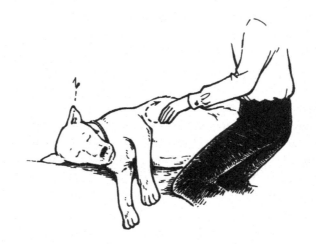

The Off Switch involves using a light touch in a circular motion.

The Off Switch is addicting! It may even make you feel calmer too! When Gus totally relaxes, you can start humming a little tune or slowly say, "Relax, relax" in a soft monotone. Do this several times a day. Slowly, the auditory cue of your humming will help Gus relax in the future when needed.

Check for problems
Doing this exercise presents a good opportunity to check for bumps, cuts, stickers, or anything else that shouldn't be there. If you find an area that is sensitive, talk to your veterinarian, there might be a problem.

"Gotcha"

Goal: To prevent annoying and dangerous "keep-away games."

It's frustrating for owners when they reach for their dog's collar and the dog backs away! Dogs do this because an owner reaching for the collar often means that something good is going to end. It keeps the dog from the delight of getting into the garbage, it stops a play session, it predicts something less than pleasant will happen (like nail clipping). You can prevent Gus from getting into this annoying habit by playing the Gotcha game. This exercise teaches your dog to anticipate good things when you grasp his collar, so that in the future, he'll be there when you really need to grab him.

Help Gus learn that grasping his collar is a good thing.

Several different times a day, gently grasp Gus's collar and then give him a yummy bit of food. To begin, do this while your dog is safely confined in your home, fenced yard, or on a leash. Stay quiet and neutral while you do this. No word ("Come," "Gotcha," "Yes") is associated with this action. The only thing you are teaching right now is that a hand on the collar predicts a good thing. Do it in a variety of situations, for example, while on a walk, or when your dog comes up for attention while you're watching TV. Do it any time your dog is hanging around you *except* when the dog is sleeping, eating, or distracted.

At first, you might need to jump start your dog by showing him a piece of food, but try not to lure him in with the food. In other words, hold the food very close to you and make the dog come in right in next to you to get it. Do *not* extend the food toward the dog—you want him to come to you voluntarily. As he gets close, gently grasp his collar. Then, give him the food. You will avoid keep away games and build lots of credit in your eventual come-when-called bank account.

Follow this sequence for the "Gotcha" exercise:

1. Gently place your hand on the dog's collar.

2. Give your dog a yummy bit of food.

3. Take your hand off his collar.

What happened to the marker?

It's okay to give food without the marker. The marker is a *conditioned* reinforcer, a bridge between the action and the food. In exercises like "Gotcha," where your dog is very close to you, I see no need for a marker, preferring just to give the piece of food. If you want to use the marker, feel free to do so. But remember that the marker is a promise you don't want to break. If you mark, you must reward.

"Let's Go," (but please don't pull!)

Goal: While out for a walk, your dog moves happily along with you without pulling on the leash.

At my training school, we teach two different types of walking with dogs: Heeling and Let's Go. They have different rules and are for different purposes. Heeling means your dog must stay closely at your side and pay attention. It's used when safety or good citizenship is an issue. We'll learn about Heeling in Chapter 7.

For now, we will concentrate on the Let's Go way of walking. Let's Go is designed specifically for relaxing walks with your dog. Your dog can do what ever he wants—sniff, potty, walk ahead, or behind you. He can be a dog and enjoy life. The only thing he *can't do* is pull on the leash. Plan on other ways to exercise your dog for the next few days—throw a ball, invite a playmate over—because you won't be getting very much distance on your walks for a while!

You won't use food or toys for this exercise. In this case, you should practice using something from the third column of your rewards chart: Interaction. Going for a walk is an interaction that is a natural reward for most dogs. Here's how we can use it as reinforcement for the Let's Go exercise.

Why does your dog pull on the leash? Because he wants to "get there." And "there" usually means somewhere out ahead of you. If you change directions, you might find that he has a new destination he feels compelled to pull toward. To make matters worse, when a dog feels tension on the leash, his natural opposition reflex encourages him to pull against the tension.

If a dog is always successful in pulling to get where he wants to go, this problem will persist until you make staying with you even more rewarding.

So, how can you use your dog's desire to move ahead of you to your advantage? Snap the leash on your dog's collar or harness and start walking. Be neutral and keep quiet. If Gus forges ahead and creates tension on the leash, stop. He'll soon learn he's not going anywhere when the leash is tight. Act as if you are a post and Gus is tied to you. Don't say or do anything. If you stick to your guns, Gus will eventually slacken the leash—probably to look around and see what's wrong. That's when the "post" comes to life and begins to move, Gus is rewarded by getting to go someplace new. If he pulls, he stays in the same boring place. If he slackens the leash, he gets to move on.

Here are some additions and variations to mix and match with the basic go/no go walking exercise above:

- You can help release leash tension by calling your dog's name once. When he looks up, the leash will slacken—you can then whip a tug toy out of your pocket and have a brief game, then walk off in a different direction. Remember, he has already learned that his name precedes good things.

- Try stepping to one side, then jiggle the leash. This will give Gus a slight sense of unbalance. If he adjusts his feet for balance, the leash will slacken. Mark and feed.

- If the leash gets tight, instead of just stopping, start walking backward, or just turn around and walk the other way. When Gus finds out you are not following and are going somewhere else with a purpose, he'll want to see why you changed direction. This might make the leash even tighter for a second or two, but he won't want to miss anything! When the leash slackens, it's reinforcement time! Continue with your walk. Gus wants to "get there."

- With Gus on a leash, put his dog food bowl on the floor on the other side of the room. Be sure Gus knows there are yummy treats in it. He can approach it as long as he doesn't pull. Let Gus figure it out.

Practice variations of these Let's Go exercises several times a day. After a bit, Gus will learn he'll only get where he wants to go if the leash is slack.

Start with puppies

Life would be so much easier if all puppies were started out with the "pulling gets you nowhere concept." And it is so much easier to teach before the dog has developed a lifelong habit of pulling!

"Helping the Latchkey Dog"

Goal: Minimize the chance your dog might become distressed when left alone.

Everyone's dog is a latchkey dog from time to time. Helping the latchkey dog is not just a matter of dog-proofing your house so he can do minimal damage. Dogs are social beings who evolved living in groups. Some dogs have a low tolerance for social isolation.

Decades ago dogs were usually able to be with us during our work day: Out to the fields with Dad, or hang around Mom and kids at the house. Then, we humans started to disappear from home. Interestingly, the tide is beginning to turn a little now with the popularity of home schooling and telecommuting! Many of the problem behavior consultations I conduct involve some variation of inappropriate home-alone behavior. Establish early in your relationship that there will be brief times when Gus will be alone. Condition him to the idea that being alone is okay by doing some of these short exercises.

Latchkey dogs sometimes engage in destructive behaviors.

Coming and going. Keep departures neutral by avoiding interactions for fifteen minutes before you leave. Leave quietly. Upon returning, walk in calmly and remain somewhat neutral for fifteen minutes. These subdued arrivals and departures are designed to make the separation less dramatic. Any attention taken away at greetings and departures should be given back at a different time during the day.

Close the bathroom door! Gus knows you won't be there all day. Stuff a hollow rubber toy with a portion of his regular daily food diet. You might surprise him with something extra special like a tiny piece of cheese in the middle of it all. Then, as you are closing the bathroom door, say *nothing*, but put the toy down outside the door for your dog to enjoy. When you come out of the bathroom, pick the toy up and put it away for next time. Be prepared to trade the toy for a treat. You can do the same when you take out the trash. He knows you'll be back in a minute.

Safety refuge—the crate. If you decide to use a crate, systematically teach your dog to accept it before ever leaving your dog home alone in it. Important details about crate training your dog appear in the Housetraining section in Chapter 5.

Plan ahead and organize a sleep-over for your dog. Don't wait until you *have* to leave your dog for a long period of time. Plan for a trusted friend to come over while you are away or have your friend keep Gus overnight or for an afternoon.

Reduce dependency. Redirect some of Gus's focus to other people, activities, and toys. Get trustworthy friends to do his favorite things with him—take him for a walk, play fetch, go for a car ride, give him his dinner bowl.

Desensitize the "I'm Leaving Now" triggers. Several times a day, grab your keys, put on your coat, then put your keys down and take your coat off without leaving.

In sight, but apart. Create one to five minute intervals when you are in one room and Gus is secured in a crate or safely tethered in a different room. Gus should be where you can see each other the entire time. It's not safe to tie your dog and leave him out of sight. Make these separation training times better by giving your dog a toy or his meal during the brief wait.

A temporary waiting station
Acquire a piece of plywood or peg board twice as long as your dog. Drill two holes in the middle, thread a leash through the holes and secure it with just enough length to allow your dog to stand and sit without tension on the leash. Place this temporary waiting station flat on the floor within view of family activities. When your dog is attached by his collar or harness to the station, he can see what's going on, but his own weight on the plywood will prevent him from going anywhere. You can make a deluxe model by putting self adhesive carpet squares on the top surface. This type of restraint should be used only for a few minutes and *only when someone is supervising.* In Chapter 7, you'll learn how

to teach Gus to go all by himself to a designated place, like a certain rug, and wait. Helpful when the doorbell rings!

A rug on a piece of plywood can be easily turned into a temporary waiting station.

"Boomerang Come"

Goal: Make coming to you fun. With the Boomerang Come game you will randomly reward Gus for running up to you.

Start in the most boring, distraction free, safe place you can think of. Your living room? Your fenced back yard? Then draw an imaginary circle directly in front of your feet. The circle should be about equal to the length of your dog. The idea is to get Gus to run into that circle from afar. You're going to reward coming, but to do so you have to get the dog to move away from you first!

You can achieve a Boomerang Come once Gus finds that entering the imaginary circle results in a great reward.

Until now we have used a continuous schedule of reinforcement (see Chapter 2) with our relationship exercises. One correct response, one reward. Dogs need a rich reinforcement history to fall back on, but, sooner or later, life happens and there might not be a reward. With this exercise we will begin something like a lottery game. Every once in a while, at random, Gus won't get a reward, but he'll get the chance to continue the game and perhaps earn a reward the next time. In other words, you will be using the intermittent reinforcement technique introduced in Chapter 2.

Begin with a hungry dog. Lure Gus into the imaginary circle by showing him you have a pouch full of his regular food and a few special treats. Show him a piece of the regular food, then say "Get it," and toss it a few feet away: Right, left, or in front. Stay still and allow Gus to chase the food. After he grabs the food, he will likely lift his head. Say "Gus, Come!" At first, you can blatantly advertise that you have a second treat waiting for him. Tap your bait bag, then show him the piece of food in your fingers. If you planned the training environment properly, he'll be there! You're the most interesting thing going on! When your dog steps into the circle, give him the special piece of food. If you'd like to mark and feed here, do so. Gus will be right there where you can slip the food into his mouth. And that's what we want, for him to come *that* close to you when he's called. So close that you can give him a piece of food without either one of you reaching!

Next, proceed in one of three ways, or vary it!

1. When Gus returns to the circle, mark and feed, then say, "Get it," and throw yet another treat in a new direction.

2. When Gus returns into the circle, no mark, no treat, tell him "Get it" and toss a treat away from you in a new direction. The cue "Get it" will actually become a reinforcement, because the game will continue and he knows you have more goodies to share.

3. When Gus returns into the circle, with his head very close to you, grasp his collar and give him a piece of food. Now you've added the "Gotcha" exercise! While he's still in front of you with your hand on the collar, throw a piece in a different direction, and then release him to "Get it."

Randomly choose these options when Gus returns to the imaginary circle. Also, vary the distances you throw the food. Don't be stingy! If you want to give him two pieces in a row once in a while, go for it! The food reinforcement is your invisible leash. It's fueling your dog's desire to come.

Do three to five sessions of this exercise a day. Start sessions in boring environments and then gradually move into more distracting environments.

Long lines

The Boomerang Come exercise works well off leash in an enclosed area. If you don't have a safe place, you can use a long line. Also known as a light line or safety line, these ten to thirty feet long leashes are an excellent transition from indoor training to training in the real world of unlimited and unpredictable distractions. They are not used to move your dog physically from place to place. Attach the long line to a harness instead of Gus's collar. If he accidentally runs to the end of the line, his neck won't be jerked.

Summing up the relationship foundation program

Once you have completed all the exercises in the relationship foundation program, you will have established a leadership role based on mutual trust—a bond. Leadership means different things to different dog trainers. For some, the word leadership is synonymous with assertiveness, aggression, dominance, and forced submission. I'd rather think of it as kind and consistent management, guidance, and communication.

A model for leadership

For several years, I had the pleasure of working with a pioneering group of reward-based pet dog trainers in Australia. I like their definition of the word "leadership." These words of wisdom are from their handbook which helps distinguish a thoughtful leader from just being a boss:

> The boss uses I.
> The leader uses we.
>
> The boss creates fear.
> The leader inspires trust.
>
> The boss knows how.
> The leader shows how.
>
> The boss relies on authority to get things done.
> The leader relies on cooperation.
>
> The boss provokes resentment.
> The leader fires enthusiasm.

Author unknown, People Pet Partnership, Australia

Chapter 5

FRAMEWORK

THE HOME ENVIRONMENT

Everyone—people and pets—are happiest in the right kind of home environment.

A successful home environment meets the needs of your dog, your family, and your neighbors. Basics like housetraining, getting along with other family members (especially kids), and being quiet and mannerly are all important parts associated with establishing such an environment. How to do this and how to enrich your dog's life along the way is the subject of this chapter.

Have a management meeting

Think of your family as a management team. As a group, you need to work together to decide what you can do to make your home environment succeed for both you and your dog. So, have a family meeting. Come to an agreement on acceptable house manners. Will Gus be allowed on furniture? Will any rooms in your house be off limits?

Think about how to dog-proof your house—making "bad" behavior difficult for your dog. What can you do to make it easy for good behavior to happen instead?

Have a meeting and decide on things like whether or not it's ok for your dog to ever be on the furniture.

After your meeting, put plans into action. Walk through your house and decide what might be tempting or dangerous. Put trash containers out of reach. Electric cords should be gathered and tucked behind furniture. Many house plants are poisonous to dogs. Put them in a safe place. Valuable or important items should be out of tail wagging reach, nose reach, or jumping up reach. Do you really need to display grandma's antique vase on the end table? Can your dog get to dangerous cleaning supplies? Your stash of chocolate can make a dog very sick. Is there a puddle of toxic antifreeze leaking onto the garage floor? Are there poisonous mushrooms in your yard? Plan how you will safely exercise and confine your pet. Allowing a dog to run at large is inexcusable. It puts your pet at risk and is probably against the law where you live. Will your yard need to be fenced? If your dog will be walked on a leash, whose responsibility will this be?

As part of your meeting agenda, identify potential problems in your house, and take steps to avoid them before they occur.

Housetraining

Teaching the dog where to toilet should be at the top of your priority list, especially with a puppy. Decide where the designated area should be. A section of your own back yard is appropriate. Select a regular potty area outside away from where people walk or congregate, but close enough to be convenient. It can be clearly designated by landscaping with decorative rocks, hedges, or a change in surface. The toilet area's surface should be easy to clean up. Think of the pros and cons of grass—residue is often left. Sand tracks in easily, pebbles might be tempting to chew and dangerous if swallowed. If you are considering bark mulch, note that some varieties such as cocoa bark mulch are toxic. Some bark, like cedar, will stain a light-colored dog.

Dogs are inherently clean animals. If given options, they prefer to separate their living and toilet areas. If you can prevent accidents during the first several days of your life together, you will be well on your way to success. The dog must be everyone's top priority. *Supervision* is most important. Unless you plan to have your dog use an indoor toilet, train the new addition of your family to use an outdoor area right from the start. Exceptions to the outdoor-toilet rule might include the very young puppy left home alone for long hours, an unvaccinated puppy, small dogs who live in apartments, or in cases where either the dog or owner is disabled. Even if you want to go outside, there may not be an appropriate outdoor space for city dwellers. In these situations, the dog should be trained to toilet on commercially available pet pads.

Be sure you are attempting to train a healthy dog. If the dog has a kidney or bladder problem or diarrhea, these matters must be taken care of before you will make much progress.

How to tell if your dog has to potty

Dogs usually defecate shortly after each feeding and urinate more frequently. Take him to the toilet area first thing in the morning, after a play period (or other stimulating activity), after a nap, and after eating. If you see him sniffing the floor and circling, he may need to toilet. Don't forget to take him out to potty just before going to bed at night. You may want to stay up later than usual while he's young so it's not such a long night.

Don't let him fool you!
Don't necessarily interpret whimpers in the night as a need to toilet. Your dog may just be looking for attention.

Scheduled feedings
Please consult your veterinarian and follow his or her instructions regarding proper diet and schedules of feeding. Experience shows that regular meal times rather than eating from a continuously full bowl will help manage the toileting pattern. What goes in on schedule comes out on schedule. Ask your veterinarian if it's appropriate to withhold food and water late in the evening. It might lessen the chances of a dog needing to go out during the night.

At the toilet area
When housetraining, always bring the dog directly to the designated area on leash. Stay with your dog until you get results. Going outdoors is full of distractions. Gus might become interested in other things and "forget" he has to toilet. Keep him on leash and slowly circle the specific toilet area to keep him focused. If he doesn't toilet within four or five minutes, go directly back inside—no outdoor play time. Then try again later, but be sure to supervise or confine him until you take him out again.

Choosing a designated area and rewarding the behavior as it happens are keys to successful housetraining.

When he does go in the right place, *wait* for him to finish, before you mark and feed or give praise. If you reward at the first sight of poop or pee, your enthusiasm might distract and interrupt the dog. The behavior you want to reward is an empty dog. Don't fall into the habit of taking Gus right back indoors after toileting; he probably likes to be outside with you. You might condition him inadvertently to take a longer time toileting than necessary so he doesn't have to go right back in when finished. Let him walk around a bit or play with him briefly before heading back inside. When you get back inside, allow your dog the privilege of roaming the house freely while you supervise. As time goes on, he'll be able to earn access to more rooms for a longer time and eventually without supervision.

Add a verbal cue

Once your dog is well on his way to successful toilet training, you can start to add a verbal cue to the action of toileting (see Chapter 6 for more on verbal cues). It only takes a bit of observation to know Gus's behavior and posture just as he's about to go. Say words such as a cheerful, "Go potty," *just before* your dog begins to toilet. In time, he'll associate this term with the urge to go. You can use "Go potty" when you're in a hurry or in a strange place that might cause him to hesitate.

Accidents

Punishment after accidents will only frighten and confuse the dog and damage your relationship. You can never be sure the dog understands exactly what he did wrong. If he made a pile in the kitchen and a couple of minutes later you smack him with a newspaper, he has only a slim chance of associating it with the accident. Spanking, "rubbing his nose in it," or sending him to exile in the cellar does nothing to help housetraining and does much to damage your relationship with your dog. Get the newspaper and smack yourself for not paying attention.

Clean up accidents, but do so when your dog isn't watching you. He might actually find this kind of attention and activity a form of reward. A commercial, enzymatic odor neutralizer will help your dog avoid the spot should there be some residual scent. Vow to be more attentive and manage things to avoid another accident.

Some dogs show signs of being housetrained within a few days. Don't be fooled into trusting those dogs. More than likely, the early success can be attributed to your being attuned to the dog's schedule of elimination rather than the dog actually taking responsibility. Continue the housetraining procedure for several more weeks.

A house within a house: The ever useful dog crate

One of the best ways to make a better home environment for your dog is to provide him a house of his own—a portable dog crate. Some people call it a kennel. It's a small box made in a variety of sizes and materials with a door. The dog can be placed in the crate, near a family member, at times when you are too busy to supervise or if you have to step out for a few minutes. Crates have been used by generations of knowledgeable pet owners, just as parents have used cribs and playpens to help them supervise their human babies. If a crate is used properly, your dog will enjoy the security and privacy of his very own "den," and can avoid much of the confusion and unhappiness of the punishment you might be tempted to administer for accidents.

Introduced and used properly, your dog will willingly go into his crate when asked.

These small, lightweight kennels are tremendously useful in supervision of your pet. In fact, you might decide to have more than one, especially if you have a young, growing dog. Are crates expensive? They are certainly cheaper than hiring a carpet cleaner or replacing broken or chewed home furnishings. They are certainly worth the peace of mind of knowing your pet is safe and comfortable when you leave the house and not chewing an electric cord or having a serious setback in housetraining. Check with grooming parlors, pet shops, or your veterinarian to borrow or purchase a crate. Mail order catalogs or dog show concessions are also good sources.

A crate can help with housetraining

It's possible that your dog might urinate or defecate in the crate once or twice. This is part of the learning process for some dogs and some soon realize it is not pleasant to be in the same area as the mess. Most dogs, however, catch on to this concept without ever soiling their crates. Keep your dog's schedule in mind and never use the crate as a substitute for taking your dog outdoors at regular intervals.

When he's not in the crate

Some alternatives to the crate for supervision: Tether Gus to your belt to keep track of him, put a bell on his collar so you will be alerted when he begins to roam around, put him on someone's lap. They'll know when he gets wiggly and he will enjoy being close to a family member. Try a temporary waiting station as described in Chapter 4 on relationships (page 56). When he is exploring the house, cut down on the amount of territory you have to watch by closing doors or use gates to block off areas out of your sight.

Size of crate

When investing in a crate, you should purchase one that is just large enough for your dog to lie down, turn around, and sit comfortably in. If it's too large, it will allow Gus a sleeping area and a toilet area.

Types of crates

Wire crates provide the best visibility for both people looking in and dogs looking out. A good quality wire crate is heavier than plastic or nylon, but they are collapsible and come with carry handles. Wire crates have maximum ventilation. They can be fitted with a cloth crate cover for privacy and warmth.

Plastic airline crates are sturdier, provide more privacy for the dog, and cut down on drafts. They are good for car travel because they offer the most protection in case of an accident. Plastic crates are more effective than wire crates at keeping moisture, dirt, and hair out of your car, but heat up more quickly compared to a wire crate.

Nylon zippered crates are very lightweight and totally collapsible. Dogs cans see out through the material. They are an aid to supervision around the house, but dogs have been known to force zippers open or chew through the mesh. There could be a safety risk if a dog is left unsupervised.

Getting your dog happy about his crate

You've probably noticed that dogs like enclosed places: Under your desk, under the coffee table, etc. Therefore, it generally will be easy for your dog to learn to be happy in a crate. Your job is to ensure that your dog learns to associate being in the crate with pleasant experiences. The crate should be used for confinement, not for isolation or punishment. Move the crate around the house to be close to a family member if need be.

You should introduce Gus to his new crate systematically. Set it up in a high traffic area of your home. Prop or tie the door open (with some crates you can remove the door—with plastic crates you can take the top and the door off). Occasionally throughout the day, when your dog is not looking, toss a couple of especially yummy treats into the crate. The dog eventually discovers these goodies which help him make good associations with the crate.

Once your dog seems to be getting used to the open crate, move on to having him in the crate with the door closed. One way to do this is to place his food bowl in his crate at meal time. If he seems worried, place it in front of the crate for the first few meals. Repeat a few times before you close the door.

When Gus is comfortable being in the crate with the door closed, try leaving him alone the amount of time it takes him to eat his dinner. One technique is to go into the bathroom to hide out for that waiting period. Closing the bathroom door behind you isn't as distressing to most dogs as going out the front door. If he begins to whine or barks, wait for at least four to five seconds of silence before you let him out. Don't reward fussing! If he is fussing, next time cut the time you leave him in the crate in half. Repeat this process several times a day with you going to a different location. See if you can build up the time he is alone in a closed crate to twenty to thirty minutes. This may take several days or longer, but it's worth the effort.

How long in the crate?

Short times in the crate should be interspersed with supervised time outside of the crate. The younger the dog, the more often he needs to eliminate. Here are some approximate time limit guidelines—for crating your dog by age:

8-10 weeks	30 - 60 minutes, longer overnight
11-13 weeks	1- 2 1/2 hours, longer overnight
14-17 weeks	2 ½ - 4 hours, longer overnight
18 + weeks	5 - 6 hours daytime, longer overnight

At about three months of age, your dog can sleep in his crate for most or all of the night.

Crates for automobile travel

It's distracting for a driver and dangerous for a dog to ride loose in an automobile. The crate should be attached to the seat of the car or floor of the van with straps. This is important because in stop-and-go traffic, the crate can slip, making the dog uneasy or frightened. A firmly secured crate can cut down the possibility of motion sickness. If there should be an accident, a loose crate flying around the car is, of course, a bad thing.

Most dogs like to see where they're going. Try to position the crate so it can be high enough to offer a view. Two exceptions: The dog who gets carsick and the dog who likes to "chase" the scenery as it goes by. These dogs might be more comfortable and/

or manageable when the crate is positioned down low or with a towel or blanket thrown over it.

The combination of hot weather and dogs left in crates inside a car can be serious or fatal. Plan ahead, know what stops you will need to make. Consider leaving your dog home on hot days—don't depend on finding a shady parking place. Someone might have beaten you to it. A dog's normal body temperature is 101.0 to 102.5 degrees Fahrenheit (38.3 to 39.2 Celsius). They do not tolerate a rise in temperature well. On a warm day, the inside of a car heats up very quickly, even when left in the shade. Dark colored cars are especially heat absorbing. On a 78-degree (25.5 C) day, the temperature inside a car parked in the shade is 90 degrees (32.2 C). It can reach 160 degrees (71.1 C) in minutes if in direct sunlight.

Kids and canines

Parents should think of three important things when it comes to kids and dogs together: 1) SUPERVISION; 2) SUPERVISION; 3) SUPERVISION!

Introducing your new baby to your dog

Most dogs get along just fine with infants, but why not do a little advance preparation for the new arrival to make sure the first meeting goes smoothly? All family dogs should be trained in basic manners. If a baby is expected, brush up on the training exercises outlined in Chapters 6 and 7. If anything else in the dog's lifestyle will change (like a new room to sleep in, or a certain room to stay out of), it should occur before the baby comes home.

As you get your home ready for the new arrival, be sure the dog gets little doses of baby. Let him watch and "help" you while you hold a doll or walk around with a teddy bear. If you are going to use them, sprinkle some baby powder or rub some lotion on the doll to get your dog used to these new activities and smells. Order a baby sounds CD to acclimate your dog to the sounds that babies make. The CDs come with instructions and tips. Introduce the dog to a blanket that has baby's scent on it before you actually introduce the baby. You could wrap a doll in it, and allow the dog to investigate this novel smell.

While many dogs and small children get along well, there are a number of things you should do to improve the odds of avoiding problems.

Toddlers

When your baby begins to crawl and walk, the situation changes and supervision is even more important. Never leave toddlers alone with a dog even though he has been friendly and tolerant toward the child. A poke in the eye, a trip and fall into the dog, or a loud scream into the dog's ear could produce a reaction from the dog that might make him whip around and knock the baby over, or worse. The natural toddler behaviors of running, screaming, grabbing, and even hugging are enough to worry some dogs. Hugging is a primate behavior that is second nature to humans and many children are taught to hug at an early age, but it can take some dogs by surprise. Hugging is not a canine thing. It's not a good way to show affection with a dog. For more on this, read Patricia McConnell's *The Other End of the Leash (2003).*

Your dog should have an area of his own—a bed, a crate, a carpet square—any easily identified quiet space where he can be by himself away from small children. The quiet space can be further delineated to family members by placing a line of tape in front of it. The quiet place should be accessible to the dog at all times, close to family activities, but out of the traffic pattern. Take the dog to his quiet place when things become chaotic and give him some treats. Over time, he will learn to escape to this area when he wants to be left alone. Respect this. Children and their visiting friends must be kept away from your dog's quiet space.

The child's safety zone

While your dog should have an area of his own, it is only fair to establish an area for the child that is off-limits to the dog. It doesn't have to be large, but your child should have a place where the dog can't pester him. Perhaps his bedroom or a corner of the living area. This can also be delineated with tape on the floor or some visual barrier that's more aesthetically pleasing. This is a space where your child can be a kid and let his toys be all over the floor without risking the dog chewing them up or destroying them. It's an aid to, but not substitution for, SUPERVISION.

Older children

Generally problems with older children and dogs arise from rough play or over-stimulation. Dogs and children chasing and wrestling can easily get out of hand. Just like children playing together on a playground, everyone is having fun, then all of a sudden someone is crying. The games were taken too far. Keep a watchful eye on your children and especially on their visiting friends who might not have been taught how to enjoy dogs appropriately. Rather than allowing the wrong games to get started, explain some appropriate interactions. There are examples of games appropriate for kids and dogs later in this chapter.

A game of hide and seek can be fun for both a dog and child, but its best to not let it turn into a game of chase.

Being safe around dogs

Appropriate interaction with the family dog is a good place for a child to practice good manners around all dogs. I wrote an elementary school program called *Prevent-A-Bite* while working for Washington State University's College of Veterinary Medicine. Here are some excerpts:

- Please *do* leave dogs alone while they are eating or chewing a toy. If you reach down and pet the dog, it might surprise and worry her. She might not want to share her snack.

- Please *do* leave the dog alone while she's sleeping or in her quiet space. After playing all day, you like to rest. So does your dog.

- Please *do* knock on the neighbor's door and ask for help if your ball accidentally gets into their yard. If no one is home, ask for your parents help. Don't
go into the yard without permission. Their dog might be present and worry,
just as you might if someone walked into your living room without an invitation.

- Please *do* always ask permission from an adult before going up to a dog, even
if you know the dog. Ask the parents if you are visiting a friend. Dogs can't
say, "I don't want to play now," but grown ups are pretty good at figuring out
what dogs are thinking.

*Always have a child ask an adult before greeting a dog, then approach the dog from the side
(not head on), and let him come forward to sniff the child's hand.*

- Please *do* approach a dog from the side, not from the back or front. It's not
polite in the dog's way of thinking. Be sure the dog sees you. Have you ever
jumped when a friend touched you when you weren't looking? Don't point
at the dog, but show your knuckles and the back of your hand. If he wants
to visit, he'll come over to you. The side of the head or under chin is the best
place to pet a dog. If the dog backs up when he sees you and looks afraid, it's
best not to pet him.

Show your child that the proper way to approach a strange dog is to turn away from him and hold out your hand.

- Please *do* keep walking past a dog in a parked car. Don't reach into a dog's car even if you know the dog. The dog may look like she wants to be patted, but she might worry that you might take something. Do you always feel like sharing your things with others?

Parents: You are the role model

While you don't want to frighten a child unnecessarily, it is important to be honest about dogs and their behavior. Take the time to show a child how a dog might communicate that he doesn't want to be petted. Don't be shy about getting down on the floor on hands and knees and acting like a dog, if need be, so the child understands what you are saying. The child can go through the routine of asking an adult if she can pet the dog. Then, the child can practice showing the "dog" her knuckles, the "dog" stretches forward just a little to sniff. The "dog" should wag his tail and look at the child with a soft face. This is the friendly dog's way of saying, "How about a pat?" The parent can then demonstrate two types of dog body language that say, "Don't pet me."

Tell the child that if the dog stands up stiff with stony eyes and a hard face, he might be angry. Don't pet the dog. It's his way of saying, "I don't feel like a pat—leave me alone." Quietly walk away. Leave him alone. Your attention may just anger him more. This body language is easy to read, even for children. The illustration of the fearful dog, as shown below, is more difficult to read.

While this dog may look harmless, he is showing fear.

Let the child know that if a dog pulls back, he might be afraid. Don't pet the dog. Don't be tempted to comfort him. Quietly walk away and leave him alone—your attention may just worry him more. Children often get into trouble when they don't realize the dog is fearful. Children love to role play. Encourage them to show this body language themselves by getting on the floor with you.

Children should be taught that if they encounter a dog who seems very angry, stand like a post. Posts don't run; they don't make any noise. They just stand still. Do the same as the post. The dog likely will sniff you and go away. If you look at the dog, move your hands, talk, or run, the dog will take more interest in you and won't go away as soon.

What children learn early can have a big impact
Children learn from adult role models and the society in which they live. Research suggests that a home with violence or abuse toward animals produces children who may grow up to be abusers themselves. Further, there seems to be a correlation between substantial animal abuse in childhood and later personal violence to humans. Studies show that children raised with intense coercion may imitate this behavior with animals and people. (www.americanhumane.org)

In the long run
The family pet will influence a child's future outlook on all dogs. Your dog's opinion of children in general will be affected by your child's actions. In a few short decades,

the children of today will be making and enforcing the laws regarding dogs. Hopefully, your child will have a clear understanding of how to live in the company of dogs.

Making the most of the time you have together

Your dog will benefit from environmental enrichment. That enrichment can take various forms, ranging from easy to complex, from expensive to absolutely free. Some of the easiest ways to enrich your dog's environment are simply to make the most of the time you have together.

If Gus were to start a list of his needs and rank the items, up toward the top would likely be companionship. Time with his people. Some of us are lucky enough to work at home or have places of employment that welcome dogs. Most of us do not. Because you are most likely a busy person with a job and human family, you will need to multitask to set aside some time to spend with your dog. Here are some of my suggestions to help make that possible.

Set your alarm earlier

This is a simple one. Get up fifteen minutes earlier than you would otherwise to go for an extra walk. It's good for you and good for your dog. Weather too yucky for a walk? How about some indoor games like fetch or hide and seek? Review the "Practice Heeling in Little Places" exercise in Chapter 7. Acquire some interactive "find the hidden treasure" puzzle boards. Puzzles are available for purchase on-line and are great ways to give your dog some mental exercise.

Tourist!

Let your dog be a tourist when you run errands. Dropping the kids off at school? Going to the drive-in bank? Include Gus on errands that don't require you to park and leave him for any significant amount of time. Not much physical activity, but a change of scenery! It will only take a couple of minutes more to stop off at an interesting place on the way home for a brief walk or training session. Your vehicle should be dog friendly and dog safe. Use a crate or a dog seat belt. The back compartment of a mini van or SUV can be adapted with a metal or plastic barrier. Stow an extra collar and leash aboard and a bottle of water. Plastic poop bags are a must. Also, put together an emergency stash of non-perishable dog treats.

Taking your dog with you while you run errands is a great way to keep him entertained when he might otherwise be left alone.

Foraging

Dogs were designed to hunt for their food. Working for dinner is still good occupational therapy. If Gus eats dry kibble, occasionally feed him dinner by tossing part of his meal down your hallway. Now Gus can have the fun of hunting for his meal bit by bit.

Fetch!

Many people play fetch with their dogs, but did you realize that throwing a toy for your dog to retrieve goes nicely with many of the chores you have to do anyway? It's actually something you can do with your dog while working at the computer, cleaning the house, or raking the leaves. Finding such a multi-tasking opportunity just takes a bit of creativity on your part. Gus doesn't retrieve? Read how to teach this skill in Chapter 6.

Spin the bottle game

Create a home-made interactive toy from a plastic drink bottle. Bore a hole on each side of the middle of the bottle and insert a dowel. A wooden chopstick works well with eight ounce bottles. You now have an empty bottle that can spin around on a dowel. Put a little dry food into it. Hold it by the handles, one hand on each side of the dowel, close to the bottle. Be sure the dowel is not sticking out beyond your fist. It might poke your dog. By now Gus is probably clambering around wondering what you're up to. Show the new toy to Gus. He will eventually nose it or put a paw on it and figure out how to spin it to get the food to fall out. Now you can watch the news and play with your dog at the same time. Put it away when you are done as it is for supervised play only.

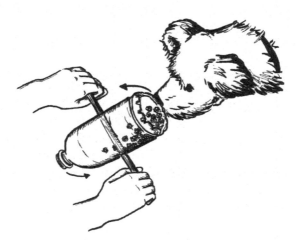

Show your dog the spin the bottle toy in action.

Inviting dogs and friends over to play group games

Most of us enjoy having friends over to our house and doing some entertaining. We do it for ourselves and for our kids. Why not do it for our dogs as well? Invite a couple of friends with nice dogs over for an evening of games. Think of games you like to play, then be creative and adapt them to include dogs. A poker party with dogs? What about dominoes? Square dancing? Consider the variables of space, personality of the dogs (and humans!), and the varying skill and energy levels of the dogs. Below are some suggestions. For more ideas, look on the Legacy website (www.legacycanine. com).

The shell game

Place three sturdy plastic bowls upside down in a line on the floor. One dog plays at a time. The game leader shows the dog that he's putting a biscuit under one bowl, then shuffles the bowls around. Have fun watching the dogs work out how to get the biscuit. If you like competition, this can be a timed event.

Pair the socks

Finally, a good use for odd socks! Go into your drawers and get a few odd socks and some matching socks as well. Select two teams at random. Try to have at least one dog on each team that can retrieve reliably on cue. Create a starting line. Place socks ten feet from the starting line in a circular pattern like the face of a clock. One team goes first, the other watches. Set a timer for a minute or two, depending on how many dogs need a turn. The dogs who retrieve are then sent to the circle, one by one, with the owner staying behind the starting line. The dog can bring back one sock of his choice. If any dogs on that team don't retrieve, the owner can walk the dog over to the circle, pick up the sock closest to twelve o'clock position, put it under the dog's collar, and walk back over the line. Next teammate goes and picks up the next sock in clockwise position and returns. Keep it up until that team runs out of time. One point for each sock. Five points bonus if you get a pair. Set up again and the next team goes. Surprise! The winning team gets to clean up after the party!

Spoon race

The dogs are on leash, a chair is positioned ten feet from the starting line. The owner has a leash, a spoon, and an egg nestled in the spoon all in *the same hand.* The dog and owner must get around the chair and back without losing the egg—a much easier task if your dog is not pulling. This is a fun way to practice the Let's Go exercise from Chapter 4. Help the owners come up with a motivational strategy to get the job accomplished. By the way, you might want to use boiled eggs or a plastic toy egg. Another less messy option is to use measuring cups and tennis balls. Competitive? Make teams. Time the event. Assess penalties.

Think your dog can walk with you without pulling? Test it out with a Spoon Race.

D - O - G

The first owner demonstrates a behavior with his dog. Example: She might ask her dog to Sit, Speak, Shake, Lie down, or Bow. The rest of the group is given one minute in which to practice this exercise with their own dogs. They then have thirty seconds in which to show that their dog can do the exercise. If a dog cannot complete the demonstrated exercise, that dog is assigned a "D." The next owner demonstrates a different exercise and the game continues. Each time a dog is unable to perform an exercise, another letter is assigned. When a dog has earned the three letters D - O - G, the dog and owner retire to a corner to do some independent practice! Last dog and owner to receive D - O - G are the winners—they have to host the next dog party.

BYOD barbecue

You can combine people fun and doggy fun by having a cook-out and inviting friends with dogs who play well together. On a hot day, you might fill a child's plastic wading pool with some water and allow the dogs to play with floating toys or just splash around. Some dogs enjoy "going fishing"—press a small hunk of cheese into a hollow rubber chew toy and drop it into the pool. It will sink to the bottom, but the dogs will have fun trying various fishing techniques to get it out. Monitor for toy and food guarders! Before the dogs become too worked up or rowdy, have a brief Off Switch session as described in Chapter 4.

Multitasking games for children, dogs and parents

If you have kids, you can be clever and time-efficient by entertaining and educating your children and dog at the same time. Children learn by doing. Instead of, "Don't do this," the child should be coached to play safe and fun games. Here are a number of game ideas.

Family fetch

This game is for a dog who already loves to retrieve. A parent, child and dog are at one end of a hallway. Give the child a small, soft ball, or toy. Something on a rope or with a handle is better than a regular ball because it won't bounce as much. There is less chance that Gus will slip in his scurry to get the ball. It's easier to get the ball back too! This is a good time to practice Stays, which are taught in Chapter 6. The adult helps Gus stay, the child throws the toy, Gus brings the ball back, the parent gets the ball from Gus and gives it back to the child for another turn.

The child throws the ball, the parent takes it back. This is a game both kids and dogs can learn to love.

Double leash walks

Children love to hold the dog's leash. Buy a bungee leash or make one from colorful elastic and then attach it to the dog's collar. The child can hold that leash during walks and the adult holds the regular leash. The child doesn't really have an effect on the dog. Parents have the added benefit of having their child on leash.

Animal squares

This starts out as an art project for the child. Help your child create two pictures each of at least five animals. If drawing is too tedious, download two copies of pictures of animals from the internet. Put the paper in plastic page savers so they can be used again. Place each set of two pictures on the floor a few feet apart. Advanced: Child or parent can print the name of the animal alongside the picture. The child chooses a card at random and then goes with her parent and the dog to the appropriate squares. The child stands, sits, or "downs" on one animal while the parent helps the dog do the same on the second copy. Reward both! The parent supervises and coaches proper interactions throughout.

Sit-Stay bubbles

A child sits on a chair with a bottle of bubble solution and wand. The parent and dog are several feet away, with the parent helping the dog to Sit-Stay. When the parent says "Go," the child blows a strand of bubbles. The parent and dog wait for the bubbles to settle toward the ground so the dog doesn't leap up and hurt himself or the child; the parent then releases the dog to go stomp on or otherwise break the bubbles. Child maintains a Sit-Stay. Repeat.

Neighborhood walk-about

Parent, child, and a dog go for a walk. The parent has a pocket full of treats. When at a corner, the parent has the dog do a Sit-Stay while he or she puts a bit of food in each hand and shows both fists to the dog. Don't forget to hang on to the leash! Which fist does the dog sniff first, right or left? If the dog touches the left fist first, give him the treat, turn left at the corner, and continue your walk until the next corner. Repeat. Child can handle the treats if appropriate.

Road trips!

We have been focusing on home enrichment, but getting out of the house is also stimulating and provides good socialization opportunities. Here are some ideas and things to consider when heading out together.

A trip to the dog park?

Off-leash play with other dogs at a dog park can be the best thing or the worst thing that ever happens to Gus. The dog park concept is great, the dog-to-dog socialization opportunities abound, but your potential inability to control the interaction between your dog and the other dogs in the park can be a drawback, especially if you are unfamiliar with the other dogs.

Here's a quick overview of what you need to consider before heading to a dog park:

- Puppies, especially those under six months old, are easily injured, vulnerable to communicable disease, and they are highly impressionable. Bad (or good!) experiences can have a lasting effect on how they view similar situations in the future.

- Accidental injuries can occur if large dogs are allowed to play with small dogs, regardless of their temperaments. Your dog can learn to be a bully or learn to be afraid of other dogs during group play. Your dog is at risk of an attack. "Let them work it out" is not good advice. Some dogs do not resolve conflict without injury to others. Do not trust this frequently heard statement from another owner: "It's okay, she just wants to play."

- Beware of dog parks that allow toys (some do, some don't). When your dog chases a ball, your dog becomes something to be chased by other dogs. This might result in injury or argument over possession of toys. If using food as a reward for a recall, you might get several dogs coming to you! This could result in arguments over the food or the invasion of personal space. Your dog might not want to share. Hot weather and wild playing can overheat dogs quickly. Playing dogs have become tangled on another's collar and suffocated before owners could help.

- If you decide to go, it's helpful if you keep walking during your visit to the dog park. This keeps the dogs moving, therefore a bit distracted from other dogs and lessens the chance of a conflict. Entry gates are high risk areas for social clashes, so stay well away from gates. Watch your dog carefully. If he is showing calming or avoidance signals and the other dogs persist, it might be time for you to go home. Make a private play date with a suitable group of dogs.

Doggy cafes

Cafes that allow dogs are a lot of fun. Be thinking of Gus's particular personal space issues and set him up for success. Bring a towel or mat for him to lie down on. Don't trust the integrity of any tie out rings provided. Keep the leash on him and hold on to it. Have him on the opposite side of your chair from the door. You have two eyes. Keep one on your dog and the other on who is coming and going. Bring food and treats and be ready to do some Off Switch work on him (see Chapter 4) if things suddenly become hectic. And be a good citizen so that we can all continue to enjoy cafes that allow our dogs.

Some cafes allow well-behaved dogs. This is a great opportunity to spend more time together.

Visiting a pet supply store

It's great when dogs are welcome to go into shops with their owners. Some of the large chains welcome dogs. Just be sure you are ready for lots of distractions and can deal with the other visiting pets. Small dogs have an advantage. They can ride around safely in the cart.

If you have to leave your dog alone—Latchkey dog strategies

As enriching as you are going to make your home environment for your dog, it is almost impossible to never have to leave your dog alone at home for some period of time. In Chapter 4, I included a list of tips to condition your dog to be okay home alone. Here are some ideas for things you can do from a home-design standpoint to make it more comfortable for a dog who has to be left alone from time to time. A feature of the environment that might seem minor or irrelevant to you might be a big deal for your dog.

Happier indoors or outdoors?

Most dogs prefer to be indoors where their people spend time, whether the people are there or not. Your goal should be to allow Gus spend at least some time indoors while you are gone—something that a little training, the right kind of toys, and well thought out management strategies can make feasible.

Fenced yard

A fenced yard for your family dog is usually a good idea. Making sure the dog has plenty of shade to retreat to on hot days is a must. Also, recognize that most dogs prefer to remain in just one portion of the yard, often near the door to the house, so be prepared for that.

Just because you put up a fence, you may not have created a secure area for your dog. Dogs can dig, jump, and climb—many are amazing escape artists. Even if they cannot get out, a fence can cause problems for your dog and your neighbors if the fence is right next to the sidewalk. Some dogs tend to run the fence line and bark at people and other dogs passing by.

Fenced yards can be an asset or can provide opportunities for inappropriate behavior.

If you are considering adding a fence, here are a few things to keep in mind. A fence that works well confining your dog during the summer months may not be so secure when snow piles up and allows the dog to hop right over it. If you (and your dog!) can see through the fence, there may be lots of things to bark at. By the way, don't trust your children or the meter reader to remember to close a gate. The only safe gate is one that's locked or nailed shut! Please remember that a fenced yard is not a substitute for a walk.

Electronic fences?
Do your research! A great deal of planning and training for both the family and the dog is necessary to make this an effective and safe option. Take a look at page 129 to remind you of the possible fallout of aversives.

Dog doors
If you have a secure, fenced yard (dig proof, jump proof, chew proof, and safe from humans with evil intentions—and in the case of my neighborhood, cougars and coyotes), invest in a dog door to give your dog a choice of locations and a change of scenery. Instead of wondering what's happening inside or outside, he can check it out himself. Worried about Gus tracking in dirt? A strategically placed carpet runner blots up most of it.

Dog window in the fence
A chain link panel in a solid fence might be entertaining. Sort of like live TV. Is the window idea appropriate for your dog? It may create a barking problem, but if it doesn't, you can keep your dog entertained.

Dog perch
A sturdy platform that can't tip over can be strategically placed in your yard away from your fence. Now Gus can jump up and get a better view of the world. Is it a good idea? It depends. Like the dog window, a platform may allow him to see more things to bark at.

Indoor window seat
A heavy tip-proof chair or small table by a window might be fun. Trouble-shoot this idea by testing it out. Is Gus excitable enough to think about jumping out? Will he see more things to worry about or bark at? Maybe you don't want your dog on furniture. You could signal "it's okay to sit here now" by throwing a sheet over the chair.

Dog walkers
Dog walkers are a great idea for most latchkey dogs. Check his or her references. And take the time to watch the walker in action along the route to see how the dogs are handled. Will your dog be walked with others dogs? How many dogs are walked together? Are they compatible or is one constantly pushed out of the way by another? A little give and take is natural, but be sure all are having a good time.

Another option is to have a friend or neighbor walk your dog. This person might be a great friend, but objectively evaluate his or her ability to show your dog a good time while maintaining control and security. Can your friend and your dog cope well with children, other dogs, or loud noises which might occur on the walk?

Professional daycare

Doggie daycares are springing up all over, especially in urban areas. These can be great solutions for latchkey dogs, but carefully interview the proprietor and observe the daycare in progress. Are large numbers of dogs turned loose together to play? Daycare should not be a place where bullies practice being bullies and worried dogs continue to be worried. Is there rest time for the dogs? Will they have down time in crates? If so, is your dog used to a crate? Does there seem to be plenty of supervision? What is the policy on barking dogs? Do they "correct" this? How? How do they handle health issues or injuries? If you are purchasing a training option, what methods will be used in training? Is there a web cam on the premises? If so, you can check on your dog from your computer.

Trading daycare

Do you have a friend with a dog compatible with yours? Compare weekly schedules and on days when someone is home to supervise, take turns inviting the other dog over.

Companionship tapes

You might want to record a tape of your family's voices and sounds of everyday household activities. The tape may help keep your dog company, but more importantly it will help mask outside noises which might cause anxiety. Some people play easy-listening music. I had one client who taped her husband's snoring. She reported that her dog prefers it to relaxation music.

Playing recordings of sounds or music that you find your dog enjoys is a good way to help a latchkey dog cope with being left alone.

Home-alone treasure hunts

Prepare several hollow rubber toys with a small yummy surprise in each. Before you leave home, hide the toys. Use some thought here, don't put toys where Gus might tip over furniture or get caught, frightened, or injured. Build anticipation for the hunt by getting him to Sit-Stay while you hide the toys. Continue the Stay while you do all the things that predict you are about to leave: Put on your coat, find the car keys, get your briefcase. Be matter of fact when you release Gus and go to work. This downplays your departure and builds pleasant expectation for the treasure hunt.

Be careful!

Rawhide chews, pigs ears, hooves, and other natural animal by-products are a big hit with dogs and are sometimes given to dogs while left alone, but dogs can get into trouble with them. The rawhide can get limp and become caught in your dog's throat. Ambitious dogs can chew through these things with alarming speed, eating so much they get a belly ache. Do you, like me, wonder about the chemicals used in the tanning process?

Chapter 6

THE MAIN FLOOR

BASIC PET DOG MANNERS

As with building a house, start with the basics. A dog who can Sit and Stay by your side has made a great first step on the road to being a great family dog.

In this chapter, we'll address two useful stationary behaviors, Sit and Down. These are skills that pet owners tend to teach right away when they get a dog. They are important! So, why do they first appear in the middle of this book instead of the beginning? Because it helps to understand dogs and how they learn before you put that knowledge into practice. The exercises from the Relationship Building Program from Chapter 4 are a great foundation for "teaching" Sit and Down. Actually, Gus doesn't need to be "taught" how to do either of those behaviors! He already knows how to sit and lie down. You've seen him do both lots of times! The trick is to get him to do them *willingly whenever you ask him to,* so let's learn to how to do that first.

Getting behaviors to happen and putting them on cue

There are many reward-based methods to elicit specific behaviors from your dog. The two most frequently used by modern dog trainers are *capturing* and *luring.* In Chapter 4, we used the capturing method in the "Catch him in the act of doing something good" exercise. For Sit and Down, we'll use the luring method which is more proactive and an effective means of teaching these behaviors. In the chapters to follow, I'll point out more strategies for getting the behaviors you want.

You may have noticed that so far I have asked you to not tell your dog what to do. This may seem counter-intuitive to you, but the cue (command) should be used only after you know the dog is capable of performing the behavior.

A *cue* is a word, gesture, or event that tells the dog that it's time to perform a certain behavior that he *knows how to do.* The rule to follow is that you don't give a cue until you are very sure the dog will do what you want. That won't take long, so you will be attaching a word to the behavior soon after you start to train what you want your dog to do. But first, just practice getting the behavior rather than chanting words your dog might not understand and might begin to ignore.

You will learn some of the most common verbal cues in the next two chapters, words like "Sit," "Down," "Heel," and "Come." A cue can be a silent hand signal instead of a word. (An example of a non-verbal hand signal would be pointing toward the floor instead of saying "Down.") When you think about it, you realize that a whole range of things can also be cues. A cue can be the jingle of car keys that produces a run-to-the-door-behavior. Life is full of environmental cues for your dog. Use them to your advantage! As an example, here are some environmental cues that you could use to teach your dog when to Sit:

Cue:	Doorbell rings.
Behavior:	Dog sits on a certain small rug.
Reward:	You open the door and Gus can greet the visitor.

Cue:	Hand on car door handle.
Behavior:	Dog sits still on car seat.
Reward:	Being released to jump out of the car.

Cue: Leash appears.
Behavior: Dog sits quietly.
Reward: Leash is snapped on and the walk begins.

Sit and Down will be taught as separate exercises with different cues. The most useful feature of both Sit and Down for the family dog is that both behaviors include a "Stay" part, so we'll be working on that as well.

Circle left, circle right—The Magnet Lure Game

For pets and their people, luring is an easy way to make a desired behavior happen quickly. The Magnet Lure Game is one I recommend to get your dog acclimated to the use of a lure. Luring is used most effectively in the beginning to *jump start behaviors*. It is then phased out later in training once the behavior and the cue are learned successfully.

To introduce this luring technique, begin your training session when Gus is alert, but not overly excited. Hold five pea-sized pieces of tasty food in your hand and be ready to feed them one by one to your dog. Hold the food directly against the end of your dog's nose as though it is magnetic. More than likely, Gus will be very willing to position his nose on the treat. Think of Gus's nose as the middle of a clock. Move the lure (still stuck to his nose) in a slow circular motion about the size of a saucer. Go slowly enough so Gus can keep up. The food needs to stay against the end of the nose, like Velcro. Remain silent. Let the lure do the work. You just want to see if your nose magnet works to get this simple head circling behavior. When Gus's nose completes this saucer size trip around the clock, mark and feed. Make sure you don't do more than one circle around the clock without marking and feeding. Once is enough! Stop and rest a few seconds.

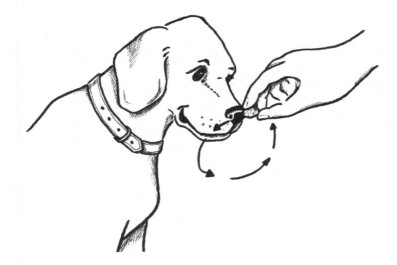

Begin The Magnet Lure Game with the treat right against the end of the dog's nose.

Then, start again. This time stop at a different place on the circle. Mark and feed. Now make the circle in the opposite direction, maybe only a half a circle. Gus will probably become expert at this in less than a day. Do three to five sessions per day, three to five reps per session for a day and you should be ready to move on to more advanced exercises.

The Sit behavior

"Control the head, control the dog" sums up the Sit exercise. When Gus's head is up, his rear will be more apt to go down. Try this yourself. Sit in a chair and focus on a spot on the ceiling just above your head. Now try to get up! Careful! Don't lose your balance. You can get up, but it's difficult! You may not have noticed, but when you get up from a sitting position, the first thing that moves is your head. You can use this principle to your advantage in dog training!

Goal: *With one cue, Gus will Sit promptly.* With minor distractions present, and no further help, he will Stay quietly in that position for one minute until released. During that minute, you are able to move away from the dog four to six feet (on leash or in an enclosed area).

Sit, step by step

There is a good chance you have already worked with Gus to teach him the Sit behavior. Even if Gus can Sit when you ask him to, please go through the motions of the following exercise. Both you and Gus will benefit from the practice of each step because other behaviors, such as Down, will be taught the same way. So, "dumb down" and go through each step. It will be fun for Gus!

Begin your training session when Gus is relaxed. Have bits of food ready in your pocket or in a treat pouch. Hold a piece in your fingers and warm Gus up by luring, marking, and feeding a couple of magnetic nose circles.

Step One: Lure the Sit! Have five pieces of food either in your hand or treat pouch. Arrange one piece between your fingers. Say, "Gus" cheerfully, then place the lure directly against his nose. Quiet! Silence please! Let the lure do the talking. When Gus is focused on the food, you're ready to start the Sit. Move the piece of food back over his head, between his ears. His nose should be like a magnet following the food. As his head goes backward, his balance will shift. Gravity! Gus's rear drops into a sitting position. Mark and feed.

Luring the dog with a treat to elicit the Sit behavior.

Sequence review:

- Say, "Gus," then be silent (don't say "Sit!")
- Magnet food lure against nose.
- Move magnet back over his head, between his ears.
- Sit happens.
- Mark and feed.

Practice three to five sessions per day until your dog is at least 80% successful.

Keep in mind:

- Please resist the temptation to say "Sit" at this point. Remember, the training rule is to *get* the behavior before you *name* it. You don't want Gus to practice listening to the word "Sit" and not responding appropriately. Getting the behavior before you name it is the best way to help Gus make the correct association.

- If Gus tries to get the food with his mouth or paw before sitting, move the food to your chest and turn your head away. When he settles a bit, try again. Please don't say "*no*" or get annoyed. Be happy Gus is so enthusiastic about training! You may want to use a less delicious food treat next time. If Gus backs up instead of sitting, train him with his rear against a wall or the couch to keep him in place.

- If Sit doesn't happen, don't worry! You haven't given him a cue, so he hasn't done anything wrong—just try again. At this point, Sit is only a variation of The Magnet Lure Game.

- Is Gus jumping up for the food? He's doing his job! He's following the magnet! The food is doing its job. It's magnetic! *Your* job is to, from the start, hold the piece of food right against his nose, so he doesn't have to reach up. Properly done, you should be getting Gus to Sit successfully in the first few training sessions of Step One.

Step Two: Cue the Sit. Make sure you are getting at least 80% success on Step One before moving to the second step. Say "Gus" to get his attention. Keep your body still. Say "Sit" just before you put the lure against Gus's nose. When the "T" is out of your mouth, move the lure to get Gus into the Sit position. When the daylight disappears between his rear and the floor, mark and feed his success!

Sequence review:

- Say "Gus" in a happy tone.
- Verbal cue "Sit," then be quiet.
- Lure the Sit.
- Sit happens.
- Mark and feed.

Keep in mind:

- Be quick with your mark and feed. Timing is important. Aren't you glad we practiced these skills earlier without Gus?
- You might want to practice in front of a mirror at home to help you know just when Gus's rear makes contact!
- Say "Sit" only once while your body is totally still. Then, produce the lure and use it to get the Sit position. All of these elements are sequential: "Gus," the cue, the luring, marking the behavior, and delivering the piece of food—no elements are simultaneous. If two events occur simultaneously, *overshadowing* might occur. (In overshadowing, one event is blocked out by the other event.) If you say "Sit" and are moving the lure at the same time, the movement of the lure may block out (overshadow) your verbal cue.

Step Three: Longer durations of Sit. Now, we will begin to build duration with this behavior. Say "Gus" to get his attention. Keep your body still. Say, "Sit" in a clear conversational tone just before you put the lure against his nose. When the "T" is out of your mouth, you can move. Produce the lure and get the Sit position as before. Remember to say "Sit" only once. This time when Gus Sits, *wait a few seconds before* you mark and feed. You can allow Gus to lick or nibble at the piece of food to keep his head up. Ping-pong between durations of one to five seconds of uninterrupted Sit before you mark and feed.

Sequence review:

- Say, "Gus."
- Clear verbal cue "Sit," then quiet please.
- Lure the Sit, focus head upward with the lure.
- Sit happens.
- Ping-pong durations of one to five seconds.
- Mark and feed.

Keep in mind:

- At this point, you might be tempted to test Gus by not keeping the lure directly against his nose. Even if you don't think you need to, do it anyway! Build a really good foundation. Go through all of the steps because we will need these same steps in the Down exercise.

Step Four: Adding Stay and Release cues. So far, you have relied on the Mark of Distinction followed by a piece of food for establishing new behaviors. With stationary exercises like Sit and Down, you will introduce Gus to a new concept, that of "continue doing it please!" Gus has already found out he can stay in the Sit position for up to five seconds. Now, we'll teach some new cues to prepare him for an even longer duration. That cue is "Stay." And finally, we will let the dog know it is all right to get up from his sit by the use of a *release cue:* "Okay." A release cue is used to let the dog know he can stop doing whatever you asked him to do. Allowing him to get up and move around will function as a reward that can replace a treat at the end of the behavior.

Sequence review:

- Say "Gus" in a happy tone.
- Clearly say the verbal cue "Sit" one time only please.
- Then lure the sit, focus head upward.
- Sit happens.
- Mark and feed.
- Say, "Stay" in a conversational tone (allowing sniffs, licks, and nibbles on a lure).
- Ping-pong short durations of three to five seconds.
- Say "Okay" in a very upbeat distinct tone, at which time he is free to do whatever he wants. The Sit-Stay is over.

Keep in mind:

- "Stay" and "Okay" are the words most dog trainers use, but they are not necessarily the best choices. Choose your words carefully. If your dog's name is Kate, you won't want to use the word "Wait" for example as "Kate, wait" could be confusing. Think of the other cues you will be using with Gus and stay away from anything that rhymes.

- "Stay" means maintain the current position unless released or told otherwise. If you give another cue, such as "Come," the release is assumed and the Stay automatically ends when he gets up to come to you.

- Saying "Good dog" and/or petting him does not mean the exercise is over. The release word means the exercise is over. As you extend duration, you may want to tell Gus he's being good, which is fine. He can receive praise or treats while in the Sit position.

- What behavior should you expect when you use your release term? It should mean within reason, to just be a dog. Do whatever. Some dogs will stay there at first, but they have an amazing capability for figuring out just what you mean very quickly.

Step Five: Fading the Lure. This means lose the use of the food as a lure—however, you continue to use it as a reward. Assuming you have done the first four steps, now is the time to bet Gus has caught on to what the cue "Sit" means—and he can do it without being lured. Now, you will keep your hand perfectly still, even if you are holding food, and say, "Sit" once. No body language, just "Sit." My money is on Gus! Bet he does it! If you get the Sit, then mark and feed, and give some generalized praise. The food doesn't release the dog. The praise doesn't release the dog. Your release word releases the dog. Be consistent about this; his life may depend on it some day! If Gus doesn't sit promptly for the first cue, just bring out the lure and help him, rather than repeating the word "Sit."

Sequence review:

- No visible food.
- Say, "Gus" in a happy tone.
- Clearly give the verbal cue "Sit" one time only please.
- Wait for Sit to happen.
- Mark and feed.
- Say, "Stay" in a conversational tone.
- Quietly give him a piece of food while he's still sitting.
- Some quiet, generalized praise is fine too.
- Say, "Okay" in three to five seconds.
- No party. You're done.

Keep in mind:

- Gus is not perfect. The only perfect dog is one you buy from the toy store. Expect some relapses here and the need to go back to the earlier steps.

- I doubt that you will be perfect as a trainer. Did you mess up your timing? Don't beat yourself up over that. Your dog will give you another chance. Smile and try again.

An important new step

At the start of training the Sit behavior, the *food lure makes Sit happen.* This is luring. Luring is okay for a jump-start. Luring is a training aid. In Step 5, you have progressed to giving the verbal cue "Sit" and when the dog sat, then the food appeared—*Sit made the food reward happen.* This is the real meaning of reward in training.

Once the dog Sits properly, he will make the food reward happen.

Building the reliability of Sit

Let's begin to work on the reliability of the Sit behavior. The key is to be a splitter and not a lumper. Don't change more than one aspect of difficulty per session. The typical variables for training stationary exercises like this are called the 4 D's. These are:

- Distance.

- Duration.

- Different environments.

- Delivery of reward.

Distance

Begin to move away from your dog as he remains sitting. To help Gus with this separation, ask him to "Sit," then say, "Stay." Turn your head away and break eye contact. Looking away is a good first step to build distance. Or, after you say "Stay," shift your position slightly as if you are going to move, or try moving away only one step. Mix it up and increase distance slowly. It's training time, not testing time. Help keep his head up by talking to him and by not going too far too soon.

Duration

When your dog is steady on his Sit-Stay for up to five seconds, try extending the duration of the exercise a little. Your eventual goal is sixty seconds, but ping-pong back and forth rather than steadily increasing the duration of Stay. When working on duration for the first couple of reps, keep your distance from the dog short and give a reward at one or more times during the position.

Different environments

Once Gus is performing well in his usual, calm training environment, now it's time to complicate matters a little by introducing distractions or taking him to a new training site. If you have been working inside, try going outside into your backyard and see how he does. Then, go back inside and see if he can maintain a Sit-Stay while you walk to a closet and put on your jacket. Want a bigger challenge? See if Gus can do a Sit-Stay during a walk in the park (on-leash, of course). When you increase the distraction level that much, make sure you decrease your distance from Gus. Don't ask for a long Sit-Stay, and keep your rate of reinforcement high.

Delivery of reward

Now is the time to start to randomize the delivery of your reward. "One-fers," "two-fers," and "three-fers" are slang terms for how many times the dog has to correctly perform a behavior to get his pay-off. It's an easy-to-remember system to help trainers move away from continuous reinforcement. Start by conducting one session where you give Gus a piece of food every other time he does the Sit properly (see page 88). This is what is called a two-fer—two behaviors for one reward. You can smile and give Gus a pat as an alternative, but it's the start of playing the food reward lottery.

More About Two-fers and Three-fers

The concept of an intermittent schedule for the delivery of reinforcement was introduced in Chapter 2, however, most of what you have learned so far has involved a continuous schedule of reinforcement. The dog does what you want and you give him a reward, essentially a 1:1 ratio of correct behavior to reward. Real life dictates, however, that we humans will not be consistent. You won't be able to reward every behavior that meets your criteria unless you and your dog live in a vacuum. You might as well learn to train with that reality in mind.

While it might seem contradictory, the intermittent or random reward method is used to strengthen a learned behavior. The dog is not able to predict just which behavior will be rewarded, but receives the reward intermittently and unpredictably. There is no set pattern. The trainer does not single out good or better responses. The reward is totally random, like playing a slot machine or going fishing. And dogs, like humans sitting in front of a slot machine or waiting hours to get a fish on the line, are willing to "work" for these more random rewards.

If random rewards didn't work, people would not fish.

Practical applications for Sit-Stay

What began as Sit has now become a Sit-Stay. The beauty of this behavior is that the dog now finds it so rewarding that you can put your dog in a Sit-Stay to minimize the chance he will engage in something else that you consider a problem behavior. You can see in the following examples how Sit-Stay competes with and takes the place of irritating habits. Now ,you can praise your dog in situations where you previously felt like punishing him!

Passing through doors

Dogs get excited about coming and going. Make it a habit for your dog to sit politely by the door until it's opened and not go through until invited. In addition to making things easier, it will prevent Gus from dashing outdoors unexpectedly and getting into the street.

Prevent this unsafe situation by working on door manners.

Sit at your side when you stop on walks

We want Gus to be a well-mannered, accepted member of your community. If you ask him to "Sit" each time you stop while walking in Heel position, it will help keep him under control and out of the way of other pedestrians. We'll learn more about Heeling in the next chapter.

Sit at the curb during walks

During walks, when you need to cross a street, teach your dog to sit before you start across. This keeps Gus under better control in busy traffic and safer should a car get too close to the curb.

Sit for attention from people

Teach Gus to sit politely when greeting people. Start by cueing and rewarding a sit when he approaches you. Gus should receive lots of reinforcement for sitting in front of a person. Should he become excited and jump up, just turn away and say nothing. Wait a few seconds and cue the Sit again. Ask your family members to do the same. When going for a walk, when someone wants to stop and say hi, take the time to help Gus sit. The next chapter has more ideas to help Gus sit calmly when the doorbell rings.

A reliable Sit behavior in all situations

Gus will soon have a strong and pleasant association with the Sit behavior. You'll be proud of him! He'll probably respond willingly and happily—until a detail changes! Sit on wet grass? That's a different behavior. Sit from a down position instead of a standing position? That's a different behavior. Respond to the word "Sit" when you are hundred feet away? He is not really *reliable* with the Sit behavior until he can handle Sit in all of these situations.

Select practice exercises from the list below. Use good judgment. Don't do anything you think might be more than Gus can handle at your current point in training.

- Before going through a door.
- During an entire TV commercial.
- When he retrieves a toy for you.
- More than once without a mark and feed.
- With you behind the dog.
- On a strange surface.
- While you gently handle an ear.
- While you sit on the floor four feet away.
- While you make your bed.
- At the same time you are knocking on the wall.
- From the down position.
- While you pick up one front paw.
- While you bounce a ball.
- While you are putting on your shoes.
- Before releasing to play with a friendly dog.
- After you put the leash on.
- Before you start going up steps together.
- During your computer shut down music.

The Down behavior

If you have taught Sit using the methods described above, the Down behavior should be fairly easy for you. The sequence of events is just about the same for both behaviors.

Goal: *With one cue, Gus will lie down promptly.* With minor distractions and no further help, your dog will stay in that position quietly for one minute until released. During that minute, you are able to move away from the dog four to six feet (on leash or in an enclosed area).

Down, step by step

Warm Gus up with The Magnet Lure Game. As before, think of Gus's nose as the middle of a clock. Move the lure (still stuck to his nose) in a circular motion about the size of a saucer. The food and Gus's nose are like Velcro. Mark and feed at random places on the circles.

Step One: Lure the Down! It may be easier for your dog if this step is done on a smooth surface so that he can easily slip into the Down position. Have five pieces of food either in your hand or treat pouch. Arrange one piece between your fingers. Say, "Gus" cheerfully, then place the lure directly against his nose. Now, keep silent please. Let the lure do the talking. When Gus is focused on the food, you're ready to start the down. Lower your hand to the floor in front of him. If your dog is attentive, his head will follow the lure. Then, pull your hand along the floor out in front of his nose. The path of your hand makes an "L" shape. In most cases, the dog's body will follow his nose and slip into a Down position. Just as Gus's elbows touch the floor, mark and feed.

Use a hand lure to get your dog to the Down position. Mark and feed.

Sequence review:

- Say, "Gus," then be silent (don't say "Down").
- Magnet against nose.
- Move magnet down and out, like an "L."
- Wait for his elbows to make contact.
- Mark and feed.

Practice three to five sessions per day until your dog is at least 80% successful for at least two day's worth of sessions in a row.

Keep in mind:

- Why settle for an 80% success rate? Why not go for perfection? These are short term goals. We will be raising the criteria soon. You don't want too much reinforcement at the lower criteria or your dog won't have as much incentive to try something different.

- Please don't say "Down" yet. The training rule is to get the behavior before you name it. We don't want Gus to practice listening to the word "down" and not responding appropriately.

- If he doesn't go down on the first try, don't worry! You haven't given him a cue, so he hasn't done anything wrong—just try again. At this point, Down is only a continuation of The Magnet Lure Game.

Step Two: Name the Down (attach the verbal cue word "Down"). When Step One is 80% successful for at least two day's worth of sessions in a row, move on. Say, "Gus" to get his attention. Keep your body still. Say, "Down" just before you put the lure on Gus's nose, then move the lure in an "L" pattern to get Gus into the down position. When his front makes contact with the floor, it's time for the Mark of Distinction. Mark and feed.

Sequence review:

- Say, "Gus" in a happy tone.
- Verbal cue, "Down," then be quiet.
- Lure the Down position.
- As soon as his elbow makes contact with the floor, mark and feed.

Practice three to five sessions per day until your dog is 80% successful for at least two day's worth of sessions in a row.

Keep in mind:

- Say "Down" only once while your body is totally still. Then, produce the lure and use it to get the down position. All elements are sequential: "Gus," "Down," the luring, marking the behavior, and delivering the reinforcement—no elements are simultaneous. Say, "Down" in a clear, conversational tone of voice. Don't be stern. Down is just another cue. Down is just another position.

- Remember to keep the lure and the verbal cue separated so one doesn't overshadow the other.

Step Three: Longer durations. When Step Two is 80% successful for at least two day's worth of sessions in a row, move on. Say, "Gus" to get his attention. Keep your body still. Say "Down." Then, produce the lure and get the Down position like before. Gus probably doesn't know the word "Down" quite yet, but please only say it once. This time when Gus goes down, wait two to five seconds before you mark and feed. You can allow Gus to lick or nibble at the piece of food to keep his head down. Do this very close to the floor. We want to assist and reward the down position.

Sequence review:

- Say, "Gus."
- Clear verbal cue, "Down," then quiet please.
- Lure.
- Down occurs.
- Focus head on floor with the lure.
- Ping-pong short durations.
- Mark and feed.

Practice three to five sessions per day until your dog is 80% successful at going Down for at least two day's worth of sessions in a row. At this point, you might be tempted to test Gus by not keeping the lure directly against his nose. Do it anyway! Build a really good foundation. It's training time, not testing time.

Step Four: Adding Stay and Release cues. Gus has already found out he can stay in the Down position for three to five seconds. Now, we'll teach a bit more duration and be clear about it. The two new terms will be "Stay" and "Okay." Just as you had decisions on what sound to use for the marker, you can decide upon the words for these new cues. There are pros and cons to those words discussed below. For these instructions, I will consistently use the words "Stay" and "Okay," but see the discussion on terms in the bullet points in the "Keep in mind" section on the next page.

The main point of Step Four is to prepare Gus for longer durations by introducing the stay and release cues. These replace the marker sound and piece of food. You will be using the Mark of Distinction and food reward again to start off new exercises in Chapter 7.

Sequence review:

- Say, "Gus" in a happy tone.
- Clear verbal cue, "Down," one time only please.
- Then lure.
- Gus goes down.
- Focus his head downward with a lure if needed.

- Say, "Stay" in a conversational tone (allowing sniffs, licks, and nibbles on the lure).
- Ping-pong short durations of three to five seconds.
- Say, "Okay" in a very upbeat distinct tone.

Practice three to five sessions per day until your dog is 80% successful for at least two day's worth of sessions in a row.

Keep in mind:

- "Stay" and "Okay" are the words most dog trainers use, but they are not necessarily the best choices. Choose all of your cue words carefully.

- "Stay" means maintain the current position unless released or told otherwise. If you give another cue, such as "Come," the release is assumed and stay automatically ends when the dog starts his Come.

- Saying "Good dog" and petting him doesn't mean the exercise is over. The release cue means the exercise is over. As we extend duration, we will want to reward Gus at one or more points during his down position, not after you have released him from the down position.

- Between practicing Sit and Down, change locations a little. Just a few steps apart is fine. Or, at times, you might want to practice Down in the kitchen and Sit in the living room. Especially in the beginning of training, this change of environment will help Gus discriminate between the two exercises.

- What behavior do we expect when we use the release term? It means, within reason, be a dog. Do whatever. Some dogs just stay there at first, but they have an amazing capability for figuring out just what we mean very quickly.

Step Five: Fading the Lure. Just as we did with Sit, it's now time to see if Gus has caught on to what "Down" means. Keeping your hand perfectly still, even if you are holding food, say, "Down" once. No body language, just "Down." I'm almost certain he'll do it for you. If so, quietly give a piece of food and some generalized praise. The food doesn't release the dog. The praise doesn't release the dog. Your release word releases the dog. Be consistent about this, a reliable response to Down is good insurance in an emergency. If Gus doesn't lie down promptly, don't say it again, just bring out the lure and help him down.

Sequence review:

- No visible food.
- Say, "Gus" in a happy tone.
- Clear verbal cue "Down" *one* time only please.
- Wait for Gus to lie down (If Gus doesn't go down promptly, quietly lure).
- Say, "Stay" in a conversational tone.

- Quietly give him a piece of food while he's still lying down.

- Some quiet, generalized praise is fine too.

- Say, "Okay" after three to five seconds.

Practice three to five sessions per day until your dog is 80% successful for at least two day's worth of sessions in a row.

Keep in mind:

- Aren't you glad Gus's cue for sit is just "Sit" and not "Sit down"? You can imagine the confusion, but some dogs learn in spite of our lack of planning ahead!

- You must be so proud of Gus by now. But don't take him for granted. Remember to keep your "Mark of Distinction" promise. If you use the marker, give the reinforcement. You might get away with it once, but eventually you'll lose the power of the mark, unless it is followed by the food.

Plan B—Emergency Downs

You may want to have a Plan B, the Emergency Down, for use when your dog is moving around. While he's walking along with you, say, "Gus, Down." Don't stop, don't ask him to sit, just get your lure out and help him. Be nice—same old sit and down tone of voice. He's not in trouble, he's in training. Build a lot of reinforcement into this before you even think about using it. Think about not having an emergency instead.

Building the reliability of Down

We'll now begin to work on the reliability of the Down behavior just like we did with Sit. Change no more than one aspect of difficulty per session. Change only one "D" at a time:

Distance

Begin to move away from your dog as he remains in the down position. To help Gus with this separation, say "Down," then say "Stay." Turn your head away and break eye contact. Looking away is a good first step at leaving. Or, after you say "Stay," shift your position slightly, as if you are going to move, or try moving away only one step. Mix it up and increase distance slowly. It's training time, not testing time. Help keep his head down by moving in quietly once in a while to deliver a reward on the floor, very close to his nose. Ping-pong distances between short and long. Take your time adding distance. Your final goal is to be able to get to the end of your four to six foot leash.

Duration

The dog is steady on his Down-Stay for three to five seconds, so now it's time to try extending the exercise a little. Your eventual goal is sixty seconds, but ping-pong back and forth rather than steadily increasing the duration of stay. When working on duration for the first couple of reps, keep the distance short and give a reward at one or more times during the position.

Different environment

If Gus performs well in his usual, calm training environment, now it's time to complicate matters a little by introducing distractions or taking him to a new training location. Will he lie down and stay if requested in an elevator? Will Gus lie down and stay by the front door while you pay the pizza delivery man? Both of those scenarios are quite challenging. Don't try for too much too soon. If you plan to work in a distracting place, keep the distance and duration short and give a high rate of reinforcement. Simply put, if you increase the difficulty of one criterion, decrease the difficulty of at least one other criteria at the same time.

Delivery of reward

Eventually you will want to start to randomize the delivery of your reward. Every once in a while, maybe once out of the three to five reps, don't give a reward. Everything else is the same. You can smile and pat Gus, but just don't deliver the reward. He's starting to play the lottery again. We'll be talking about other variable schedules and their specific uses a bit later. Start with random two-fers for now.

"Down" vs. "Off"

"Down" means to lie down. Don't confuse Gus by saying "Down" when he is jumping up on you or when he is on the furniture. Try "Off" for that instead, unless you are really expecting him to lie down. You know the situations in which your dog is tempted to jump up on a person. Plan ahead and substitute that jump with a highly rewarded Sit. Start teaching the concept of Off by placing him up on something, perhaps the bottom step of the stairs. Say, "Off" and toss a piece of food to the floor.

An optional Down position: The relaxed "Macaroni" Down

Most people are just happy that their dog is in one spot. Many dogs go down into the sphinx position—elbows touching the floor and rear legs folded straight under their bodies. That's fine. Some dogs prefer to push their back legs out, froggy fashion. In Japan, the dog trainers call this position the "Space Shuttle." Some dogs naturally flop their back hips over. I call this the Macaroni Down because the dog's back bone looks like macaroni. Some trainers think the dog is less apt to pop back up if his legs are not right under his hips.

To achieve the Macaroni Down position, once the dog is down, move the lure along the floor toward his hips. His hips will flop over into a more relaxed position.

If you would like to encourage the macaroni position for your dog's down training, that's fine. It's easy to do with a lure. After you finish the "L" shape, keep your food magnet on Gus's nose. Draw it along the floor toward his hip. His nose will follow it and his hips will turn, flopping his rear over into a relaxed position. When he gets to the macaroni position, mark and feed. Which way should you draw the dog's nose? Around his left shoulder or his right shoulder? Spend some time observing your dog while he's hanging around the house. He might have a preference! When you get him into the L, see if his body is leaning one way or the other. Go with that direction! Or just try one way and see what happens. Don't be in a rush. Make sure his nose stays on the piece of food.

You can experience the mechanics of the Macaroni Down yourself: Point your nose over one shoulder, now lower your nose over your shoulder as if you wanted to touch your ribs. Do you feel your hips rolling?

You can make Macaroni Down Gus's standard Down position. If you're ambitious, you can train it separately by giving them separate cues. Just remember, get the behavior before you name it!

Chapter 7

THE SECOND FLOOR
MORE USEFUL BEHAVIORS

The bond between you and your dog will continue to grow as you expand your reward-based training exercises.

In Chapter 6, you learned how to teach and reinforce stationary behaviors. We also practiced getting varying durations of Sit and Down. Gus gets rewarded for staying in one place and in one position. In this chapter, we'll describe several more useful behaviors, this time involving movement:

- Come-When-Called.
- Heeling.
- Station training (moving to a specific place or "station").
- Retrieving.

Elements of all of these behaviors were introduced in Chapter 4 as part of the Relationship Building Program. By working on exercises like "You Called," "Let's Go," and "The Boomerang Come," you and your dog already have a good head start on the behaviors that follow. Please review and practice those foundation exercises before you move on.

You will notice that I will not be providing detailed step-by-step instructions to teaching these new behaviors like I did in Chapter 6. Why? Because by now, you are a competent trainer! You have learned about how to reinforce the behaviors you want, you know when to add a cue, you know about rewards. So, from here on, I will just highlight some key points about each behavior and the rest is up to you!

The Come-When-Called behavior

Goal: *Gus will run up to you on the first call.* He'll be able to ignore minor distractions and quickly get close enough for you to touch his collar.

It would be great to think that when Gus is running freely off leash he will return to you in a flash as soon as you say "Come." This is, however, unrealistic for some dogs in some situations. But, you can greatly increase the odds that he will Come-When-Called by following the exercises below.

A note on safety

It's my experience that there is no such thing as a 100% reliable response to "Come." Don't bet your dog's life on your ability to get him to come back, especially if he shows a strong inclination to chase things. In real life, you never know what combination of distractions or other situations will compete with his compliance to the "Come" cue. Years of total success at having Gus come when called may give you a false sense of security. *Therefore, I strongly recommend that the following exercises should be done on leash or in a safely confined area.*

Training exercises for Come-When-Called

First, review the "Boomerang Come" exercise in Chapter 4. In that exercise, you learned to draw an imaginary circle in front of you. When your dog comes to you and crosses over the boundary of the circle, that is the point where you want to mark and feed him, or boomerang him away from you to set up for another come. You can use your release word to let Gus know he is free to move around again, or give him another cue to perform some other behavior.

Here is a menu of exercises. They are in no particular order. Read them over one by one and choose some or all to add to your Come foundation. Start with exercises that you think will be easy for you and Gus. By the time you work with Gus on all of these concepts, you will greatly increase his reliability at coming when called.

Opportunity Comes

Are there times during the day you can say "Come," because you know for sure Gus will do it? How about when you reach for the leash, or car keys, or a tennis ball? Take advantage of these opportunities by saying "Gus, Come" just as he alerts and starts toward you. If Gus is super fast and he's already at your feet, take a step backwards and say, "Gus, Come" just before he closes the gap. Follow through. If he comes, go for a walk, take him for a ride, or throw the ball. By doing so, you make coming to you as rewarding as possible.

Do the "Gotcha" exercise

In Chapter 4, you were taught to grasp Gus's collar and deliver the reinforcement very, very close to your body. You can add this sometimes to your Come exercise. When you practice calling Gus to you, grasp his collar, and give him a yummy piece of food.

A self awareness exercise: It's the pits—can you do it?

Place a coin in each of your arm pits. Now call your dog! No reaching! The point is we want *Gus* to come to *you*. Close to you. When he arrives, is he close enough that you can touch his collar without losing the coins?

My human does magic

Before you go on a walk, put something great in your jacket, then sneak out without your dog and hide it in a tree or on a fence. A ball on a rope, or a portion of Gus's next meal are options. Then, go out together, and when you arrive at a good place near the surprise, cue "Gus, Come." Give him the hidden reward! This will keep Gus guessing about your ability to produce rewards.

Vacuum cleaner comes

Almost any practice variation of Come can be even more exciting for your dog if you alter it occasionally with a "vacuum cleaner come." To do this variation, say "Gus, Come!" then back up a few steps or turn and run a few steps. Check behind you first so you do not trip. It is almost as if you have created a vacuum and the dog is sucking right up to you! Reward!

Get a distraction helper

Have a family member or helper hold Gus by the collar, talking to him and petting him, as you walk a short distance away. Then call. Your helper should let go. If Gus decides to stay with your helper, she should turn her back to Gus and remain neutral—no talking, no eye contact, just stand like a post. I'll bet Gus will run right up to you, if you've done your homework!

The leash lottery

Before it's time to leave the park, call Gus to you, reward, say your release word, and let him go again. You might snap the leash on, then take it off again and let him go back to play. Don't let the word "Come" always mean the end of fun—that the leash is on and so, now you go home.

Emergency use only

If you work on strengthening Gus's "Come" cue and practicing good management with leashes and fences, you'll avoid emergencies. But what if Gus *does* get loose accidentally? Chasing after a dog almost never works. In an emergency, try running away from Gus, he'll think he's missing something. Try opening a car door. Gus might come over and hop right in. Pretend you see something interesting on the ground! Your neighbors will think you're crazy, but start talking to a piece of grass! Be dramatic and convincing and Gus might come over to see what's going on. Grab him. It's an emergency. These measures will probably only work once, if at all. Dogs quickly become wise to this type of thing. Vow not to be placed in that situation again.

Keep in mind:

- **It's training time, not testing time.** Until you have built up a lot of reinforcement history for Come-When-Called, it would be counter-productive to call Gus when he's not apt to come. Refrain from that temptation. For now, don't call him away from something fun. If he's in the trash, go get him instead of testing your come cue.

- **Avoid "drive bys," reward Comes!** Set your dog up for success—and remember to reward that success. Once in a while I see a pet owner call her dog, the dog makes a great effort to get to that magic circle in front, but then pauses and runs off to something more interesting—what I call a drive-by. Maintain three seconds of focused reward when Gus gets to you. At that point in time, you are competing with every other interesting thing in the environment. Be sure you come out on top.

Rewards—money in the bank

You are now making deposits of motivation in your Come-When-Called account. Later, you will be able to make withdrawals—with interest! Gus is going to love to come when called!

- **Calling from a Sit.** It's not very often that a dog is sitting waiting for you to call, so don't fall into the convenient habit of practicing that way. Set up a training session where Gus is up and about in a somewhat distracting situation. Be careful when choosing distractions—you need to win this game most of the time.

- **Tone of voice.** People tend to raise their voices when saying "Come" (or "Down!"). Dogs often wonder what they did wrong. It's just another cue. Use the same medium, clear, pleasant tone of voice. Motivation will get the dog to come, not intimidation.

- **Avoid cheerleading.** You want to be enthusiastic when you call your dog. However, you don't want Gus to learn to pause and wait for your entertaining antics to start, before he shifts into gear. Praising him while en route might be okay once in a while, but try to save the high key enthusiasm for when he reaches you.

- **Posture when you give your cue.** If your dog is small or nervous, stoop down and turn sideways slightly, it might be more welcoming than bending over or stretching toward your dog.

Sit on arrival? Or not?

It depends on your preference, but be sure to get a happy, reliable response to "Come" first. Keep it separate from "Sit" for now. If you want your dog to sit after he comes to you, put them together later. There are benefits to having the dog sit after he comes, it helps him focus and stay still while you put the leash on or decide what's going to happen next.

The Heel behavior

Goal: *On one cue, your dog will stay very close to your side while you are moving together.* The dog will maintain that position, regardless of your direction or pace. If you stop walking, the dog will sit next to your side. Generations of dog trainers have used the word "Heel" as a cue for their dog to walk closely by their side. Consider using a friendlier cue such as "Side" or "With me." We will use the term "Heel" in this book.

Back in Chapter Four, we learned the "Let's Go" exercise of loose leash walking. "Let's Go" is the cue recommended for a leisurely, informal stroll with your dog. The only requirement for that cue is "don't pull on the leash." "Heel" cues a more attentive and precise style of walking together. In the course of a normal walk with Gus, you will find the need to switch back and forth from the Let's Go mode to the Heel mode. Here's an example: You're out for a walk in the park. Gus is meandering at the end of his slack leash, sniffing, looking around, just being a dog. All of a sudden, you see a class of kindergarten children bouncing and giggling toward you. They are returning from a field trip and they all have ice cream cones. With the cue "Heel," you should be able to get Gus past the kids without a mugging. Then, you can revert to the Let's Go mode and enjoy the rest of your walk.

Try not to think of "Heel" as a perfected version of "Let's Go." They are two separate concepts, each having different cues. They are used in different situations. When switching from "Let's Go" to "Heel," use your cues clearly and appropriately so that Gus gets the message in black and white.

A dog walking happily with his owner in a perfect Heel position.

Definition of the Heel position

Imagine that you are wearing a pair of jeans. Gus's nose shouldn't fall behind the seam of your pant leg, and his shoulder shouldn't be ahead of the seam. No matter which way you are moving, Gus will strive to keep in that position. Gus should be paying attention to you, with no more than a glance at distractions. Draw an imaginary circle around Gus's head when he's in this position. Gus's head should remain inside that circle. Some owners teach the dog that if his head is anywhere outside of the circle, he's subject to correction or punishment. This might be done with a choke chain and a jerk of the leash. I prefer to motivate the dog to *want* to be inside the circle by rewarding him for being there.

Most dogs are taught to walk on the left side of their people. Performance events might require left or right sides, depending on the exercise. If you walk on roads without sidewalks, you might want Gus to switch sides so your body helps block traffic. Choose one side for now. You can train the other side later with a different cue.

Teaching the Heeling behavior using target training

I've had the best success teaching the Heeling behavior using *target training*. For Heeling, target training involves having Gus touch his nose to your fist. Where the fist goes, the dog will follow.

Using your fist as a target

This exercise combines both luring and targeting. We'll use the Mark of Distinction (mark and feed) to teach this behavior.

Sit in a chair with Gus nearby. A leash is optional if you are in a secure area. As Gus watches, conceal five pieces of food in your left hand (right hand if you are teaching your dog to walk on your right). Hold your fist so your folded fingers are less than two inches from Gus's nose. He will naturally try to sniff your hand. You'll be tempted to help by touching your fist to his nose, but let him do the work and reach for your fist. When his nose touches, mark and slip him a piece of the food. Then, take your hand away and put it out of sight, behind your back. During the training session, make your target fist visible only when you are ready for Gus to touch. If he doesn't touch within three seconds, take your fist away and hide it again. Gus has missed his chance for a reward. This will help him be more attentive! That's one rep. Repeat with your hand in a slightly different location until all five pieces of food are gone. Here's a recap of the sequence:

- Present the fingers side of your fist.
- Wait for Gus to touch.
- Mark.
- Feed from your target fist.
- Take your fist away.

Repeat for a few sessions, then try two-fers—every other touch, withhold the mark and feed. That's two complete reps, but now Gus is giving you one of those for free. Try three-fers—two out of the three times Gus touches, you don't mark and feed. Ping-pong back and forth one-fers, three-fers, two-fers, three-fers, etc. Mix it up so that the reward for touching is now random.

Also, try some sessions of presenting your target fist, but move it three or four inches away so Gus has to work a bit harder to make contact. Be consistent with your target fist. Reward Gus only for touching the finger side of your fist.

Now progress to an empty fist target! Your dog sees the same picture, but now that fist is empty. The food is in your pouch or pocket. Gus touches your target fist as usual, you mark as usual, but now the piece of food comes from somewhere else. You can use either hand to get the piece of food for your dog. We're making sure he understands the target touch and is not just following the food.

Work on Heeling in this fashion in short segments of less than fifteen seconds. Slowly, ping-pong distance each rep and then increase the duration of the exercise.

Target training
In general, target training means teaching your dog to touch an object with his nose. But, you can have him use other parts of his body as well. A foot example: You could teach Gus to touch his foot to a piece of duct tape as a target. It's then possible to place the tape on any object you want him to touch with his foot. A rear end example: In this chapter, you'll be teaching Gus to sit on a target rug.

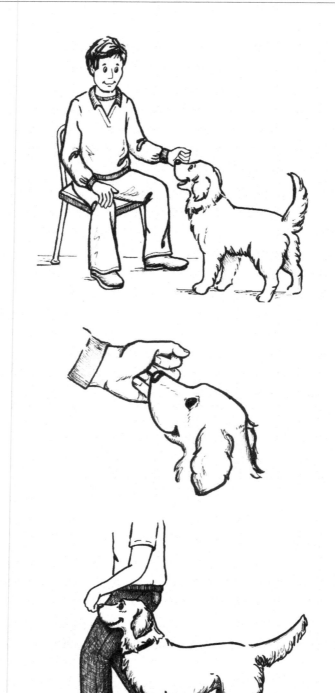

Using your hand as a target is the best way to teach the Heel behavior.

Adding the cue

This is the easy part. As Gus becomes smooth and successful at staying by your side, say, "Heel" an instant before you present the target fist.

Fading the target fist

The target fist is a training aid, not a permanent cue. Over time, you can begin to return your fist to a normal position. Gus will get into the habit of maintaining the Heel position and will not have to rely on the target fist. Just make sure you continue to mark and feed him periodically for the appropriate Heel position (see page 110).

The target stick

An alternative to using your fist is a telescoping rod with a clicker attached to the end. You can teach your dog to touch the little ball on the end of the stick. This is especially good for teaching Heel position if you have a bad back and a little dog!

Your dog will learn that touching the end of the target stick is rewarding.

Building a reliable Heel and Sit behavior

You will likely often need or want to stop when walking with your dog in the Heel position. It will be convenient if Gus sits at your side when you stop. To train this, find an unobstructed vertical surface—a wall, a couch, or a fence. Stand with your heeling side close to the surface and present your fist so that Gus's head is within the imaginary circle at your side. You've made a sandwich—the wall is one piece of bread, you are the other. Gus is the cheese in the middle. This helps Gus focus, eliminates 50% of the distractions, and keeps him straight! When Gus touches the target, move it back over his head just like we moved the lure when we taught him to sit. It's okay to say "Sit." When he does so, mark and feed, tell him to stay, and remove your hand. You're teaching him to sit close to your left side in Heel position.

Make a sandwich between you and a wall to help practice a Heel and Sit behavior.

Now you are ready to start walking again. Take a step or two as you present your hand in Heel position. You will be tempted to say "Heel"—but no "Heel" cue yet. Let your target do the work. Gus will be walking along at your side! Give Gus a break after every session (three to five reps). Use your release cue to be sure he knows he's off duty. Let Gus have a brief rest. At subsequent sessions, vary the number of steps you take, sometimes more, sometimes less. When you stop, Gus should sit. He'll learn to do this automatically very quickly. His only cue is that you have stopped. You probably won't need the lure or the verbal cue to sit.

The Heel and Sit position.

You'll be tempted to fall into the habit of marking only the Sit behavior. Sit has already been heavily reinforced. Try now to give the majority of rewards for actually keeping his head in the circle while you are walking.

Practice Heeling in little spaces

Using chalk, draw some six to eight foot long letters or numbers on your driveway. A, B, C, D, 8, 4, etc. Then work on having Gus Heel along the outline on the figures with you. It will create teamwork as you twist your body here and there and Gus adapts. You can tell where my students live—they have letters mown into their lawns! Make up your own rules. Maybe when you come to an intersecting line on a letter, you can stop and sit before proceeding. For the Figure Eight, use two obstacles to mark the middle of each loop. Eights are good because there is an automatic acceleration and deceleration needed by Gus as you round the different loops. This set up also teaches Gus to stay by you instead of going around an obstacle while on a walk.

The Station behavior

Goal: *On one cue, your dog will go promptly and willingly to a particular target rug. He will sit and remain there quietly, awaiting further instruction.* Having the ability to send your dog to a station—a designated place such as a small rug—is a means of instant, short-term control. Trainers preparing animals for movies use stations all the time. A common use of the Station behavior is to prevent a dog from causing chaos when the doorbell rings. The cue I recommend you use for this behavior is "Rug."

Choose a small area rug just about Gus's size. This "magic carpet" is the station target, it should be different from his bed or crate mat. By now Gus's Sit-Stay should be reliable. To be sure, go back and practice the sit fluency exercises in Chapter 6, but this time practice on Gus's rug.

The Station behavior, a Sit-Stay on a rug.

When he is sitting on the rug consistently, it's time to change the cue from "Sit" to "Rug." Put the rug a couple of steps in front of Gus. Walk him over and when he's standing on it say, "Rug" and pause. He'll probably understand and sit. Since this is a new cue, help him, if need be, by following the word "Rug" with the word "Sit." Mark and feed.

After he understands the new cue, try saying "Rug" when he's just a few inches from it. Throw a piece of food on the rug, he'll go! When he eats the food, pause. I'll bet he sits. If not, lure or cue him to sit. Repeat until he's willingly stepping on the target and sitting on cue.

Pick up the station rug after each rep and put it in a slightly different location.

Review the Four D's in Chapter 6 and implement them with the station exercise. The first D, distance, is an important one. You might be tempted to move the rug too far, too soon. Increase the distance Gus has to travel very slowly. Ping-pong back and forth on distances so he can gain confidence by having some "easy" reps now and then. Vary the duration of the sit. Use your release word when you want to end the exercise. Different environments: Place the rug in different locations including distracting situations. Don't go for the doorbell yet though! See the next section on door desensitization first! Delivery of reward should be random. Go over to Gus during his Sit-Stay and give him calm praise or a food treat.

Pick up the rug and put it away after each training session. This keeps the learning experience fresh and interesting.

The Retrieve behavior

Goal: *Your dog will happily go to an article placed or thrown at least six feet away, pick up the article, and return it to your hand.* Teaching Gus to fetch opens up all sorts of opportunities for new games and tricks. A session of playing fetch is good physical exercise and is fun for both of you.

Teaching the Retrieve

The retrieve is best taught by using a method called *shaping*. Shaping works well for behaviors like the retrieve that involve several steps. Think about the three things the dog needs to learn to do a retrieve:

1. Show an interest in the article that he will retrieve.

2. Go and get the article and grasp it with his mouth.

3. Bring it back to you and release it.

To build interest in what you want him to retrieve, we'll add an element of luring to the exercise. Choose a clear, plastic article that can contain food and be closed securely. It needs to be small enough so Gus can grasp it easily with his mouth, but large enough so he can't swallow it. You want him to be able to see the food, but realize that he needs your cooperation to get it out of the container. Things that work well include small plastic food containers, a clear plastic zippered coin or pencil case, or a tooth-brush travel case. An item that has a handle such as a cosmetic pouch may be easier for your dog to pick up. Be sure your dog can't get into the container without your help.

Allow Gus to watch you put some yummy food into the article. Make a big fuss about doing so. Hide the article in your pocket inside of your shirt or behind your back. Bring the article into view about twelve to eighteen inches from Gus's nose. Mark any interest Gus shows in the article—a glance, a stretch, a turn, a sniff. Take a piece of food directly from the container to reward Gus. Do this three to five times to build his interest in the container.

If Gus totally ignores the presentation of the article, say nothing. Remain neutral and put the article back. Gus missed his opportunity for a reward. No Mark of Distinction, no reward this time. Take it slowly, no more than five reps in a session, three to five sessions a day.

Progress toward your goal slowly. Think of a ladder. The goal is at the top. You will get there one rung (step) at a time by rewarding better and better attempts at the goal. For example, if Gus starts out by looking at the article, stop reinforcing looks and wait for him to move his head or step toward the article. Raise the criteria very slowly so that Gus can be successful and have a high rate of reward. When Gus is about 80% successful at this rung (the rule of thumb for moving ahead), raise your criteria again.

Building a complex behavior

Shaping is the term used to build a new behavior by selectively reinforcing variations in existing behaviors. Watch your dog. If you see something you like and could build on, mark and feed the instant that behavior occurs. Next, wait for a variation of that behavior to occur that is closer to your goal. Mark and feed. Raise your criteria slowly to make sure the rate of reinforcement is high.

Sometimes a dog will perform a couple of steps beyond what you had expected, be prepared to mark and feed. Sometimes, things go slower than expected. If Gus appears to be "stuck," simply split your criteria into even smaller increments. If the behavior deteriorates, just go back a few rungs of the ladder for the next rep. As he starts to progress again, apply the four D's and add a cue.

The ability to shape behavior and overcome problems while teaching complex behaviors truly illustrates the art of dog training. By now you are experienced at the training sequences. You will eventually get to your goal. The Retrieve behavior will be reliable and you and Gus will have even more fun.

Chapter 8

REMODELING

FIXING PROBLEM BEHAVIORS

Even though you've done your best to create a friendly, obedient dog, you might find that you need to do some remodeling along the way.

There are very few problem dogs. A dog labeled as a "problem" is usually doing normal doggy things—but from your point of view—at the wrong time and place. As with other aspects of life, when things are not as we hope, we look at our remodeling options. When the canine and human lifestyles get out of sync—or when dogs and humans don't see eye to eye on appropriate behavior—it's time to get busy and see if a change, or at least a compromise, is possible.

Solve this puzzle first

Regardless of the behavior problem you are experiencing with your dog, there are a common set of questions (think of them as puzzle pieces) you need to ask before doing a complete analysis of any behavior issue. You will need enough information from each area to fit together an appropriate remodeling program. For example, think of a family consisting of two adults who work outside the home and own a dog with home alone issues. Their remodeling program will be different from what a family with one adult and two kids who are at home all day might choose. Or, consider another family who lives with a high energy dog, compared to a family with a dog who is content to lie around and watch the world go by. When your dog is being a "problem," ask yourself these types of questions:

- **The problem.** Objectivity is needed to clearly identify the cause of the problem. Sometimes you can get a more objective opinion from a neighbor or friend who knows the dog and the dog's environment.

- **The dog.** What size? What breed type? High energy or low energy? What sort of temperament? Training history? What is the relationship between your dog and your family?

- **Lifestyle.** Does the dog stay home long periods of time alone? Is your family active with the dog? Do you take him on lots of outings? Does he stay indoors or outdoors? Where does he sleep at night?

- **The owner.** What are you and your family capable of doing with the dog? Please be realistic. Whatever you determine you need to do to address the problem needs to include a program the entire family can comply with wholeheartedly.

Document the issue: What's really going on?

Let Gus tell you what is going on by closely observing him. It will help to have your entire family document the troubling behavior. Place a notepad in a convenient location. Encourage your family members to jot down random details of Gus's behavior for several days. Focus especially on what happens to trigger the behavior. If the behavior occurs when no one is home, spy on Gus by setting up a tape recorder, camcorder, or web cam in a safe place while you're gone.

Document the problem by carefully observing what your dog is doing.

As an example, let's say you have an issue with Gus's barking habits. Here are the kinds of questions you need to answer to help you figure out what's going on with your dog:

- When does the behavior occur?
- How long has it been going on?
- Has anything changed in your lifestyle since the onset?
- Is there any pattern to when Gus barks?
- Does he bark in the morning, on the weekends, when alone?
- What is the duration of the bark?
- Are there breaks in between barking sessions?
- How long are the breaks?
- What is the intensity of the behavior?
- Is it loud or soft? Strong or weak?
- Six barks per minute or sixty barks per minute?
- Where does the behavior occur?
- Is Gus in the back yard when he barks or is he inside?
- Is there a certain room in which he barks?
- Does he bark in your vehicle?
- While it's parked? While it's moving?
- Who is present when the behavior occurs?
- Does Gus only bark when he's alone?

- Does it make any difference who is with him?
- Are there other pets in the home?
- Was the dog rewarded in any way for the behavior?
- What have you tried so far?
- How has it worked?

It may take some creative thinking to figure out why Gus is shredding newspapers.

Establishing behavior goals—breaking them down

After reviewing the puzzle pieces and documenting the problem, make sure your training goals are simple, clear and realistic. Try to work on one thing at a time. Let's say Gus is bothering the family at meal time. You might want Gus to: 1) go somewhere else; 2) be quiet; 3) keep still; and 4) not paw at your leg for attention. That's four separate behaviors, each one of which could be broken down into even smaller behavioral components. Planning your goal for Gus should include a picture of what you want him to do instead! Lying quietly on a mat against a nearby wall is an example.

At times, dog training goals will be obvious, but, at other times they will be vague. For instance, is it okay if Gus barks at a strange noise in the middle of the night? Is it okay if he whines? How about just one bark and then getting quiet?

Getting help
You should be able to solve most of the behavior problems you may encounter using the "remodeling plans" that follow. However, some problems—especially those that are more serious, like aggression or separation anxiety—may require you to get outside, professional help.

Getting started on your remodeling plan
Your first step should be to review some of the topics covered earlier in the book, such as the following:

Review health status
A health problem could be a contributing factor to, or the entire reason for, inappropriate behavior. Take a look at the information in Chapter 1 to make sure you can rule health issues out. If you suspect a health issue may be the cause, talk to your vet and tell her what's going on behaviorally with your dog. Take a multidisciplinary approach to your dog's well being. Health care and behavioral care often go hand in hand.

Review relationship exercises
To set the stage for successful behavior modification, always look back at the general foundation work covered in Chapter 4. Certain parts of the Relationship program might need extra reinforcement or adjusting before you go on to specific tools to address a particular problem behavior.

Review basic manners
You'll want to be sure Gus has a strong reinforcement history on behaviors like Sit, Down, Come, Heel, and Station so they can be used as alternative behaviors to replace some of the problematic ones. If he sits and gets a reward instead of jumping up on you and getting hollered at, everyone will be happier.

Management
Management is simply doing what you have to do to prevent Gus from practicing the inappropriate behavior. It usually involves changing the dog's environment so that he won't be tempted. While management can be very effective, in many cases it is just a temporary fix or stops something from getting worse. Think of it as first aid. However, it can buy you time to do some comprehensive training that will resolve the problem on a more permanent basis. Here are some examples of management in action:

- **Issue:** Your dog tears up mail when dropped through the slot onto the floor.
  Management: Cancel home delivery and pick up your mail at the post office.

- **Issue:** Your dog is afraid of children.
  Management: Arrange for the cub scouts to meet at someone else's home.

- **Issue:** Your dog doesn't get along with other dogs.
  Management: Don't go to the dog park.

Your remodeling toolbox: YESTRAIN

There are a number of specific tools to consider in remodeling a dog's behavior. I use the acronym YESTRAIN to remember them. Which of the YESTRAIN approaches you choose will depend on the problem you face and how you prefer to deal with the problem. Depending on the situation, you may use one, a few, or all of these approaches:

Yield a little.

Eliminate the cause or trigger.

Systematic desensitization.

Take away the reward.

Reward an incompatible behavior.

Acclimate the dog.

Improve the dog's association.

No need for nasty stuff.

Yield a little

Sometimes giving a little makes for an equitable living arrangement. Often overlooked as an option in dog training, a compromise can be an easy and effective solution. Yield a little appeals to owners with little time, talent, or inclination to train. If you work through the problem instead of trying to stop it outright, you lessen the chance that your dog will simply transfer to another annoying habit.

Here are some examples:

- "OK Gus, you can have your own piece of furniture, but stay off the others."
- "I can't walk you as much as I'd like, but I will hire a dog walker."
- "You can't dig in the lawn or flower bed, but I'll allow/train you to dig in this corner."
- "Gus, stay off the bed, except when I cover it with this old quilt."

Eliminate the cause or trigger

Taking away the cause or trigger of an unwanted behavior seems too simple a solution, but it's also a quick and effective intervention. One must be sure, however, to make the correct assessment of the situation, including the identification of the trigger or cause. There may be a combination of stimuli that provoke the behavior and you'll need to peel them away like layers of an onion. Eliminating the cause or trigger is quick and, when used appropriately, solves the problem forever and without stress to owner or dog. Bear in mind however, that eliminating the triggers may resolve one specific issue, but may not generalize to other similar situations. You may put your shoes away at home, thus eliminating the trigger of chewing, but will Gus be tempted to chew something else?

Here are some examples:

- "Hello neighbor? Your child is pestering my dog again, please come take care of him!"
- "Gus, are you growling when I pat you on the head because you have an ear infection? I'd better take you to the veterinarian!"
- "Well, Gus, I guess I'll keep the trash can in this latched closet from now on."
- "Gee Gus, you're destroying the house while I'm away at the office because you have too much energy? I'd better create some activity for you before, during, and after work."

Systematic desensitization

Systematic desensitization is a technique frequently used for fear responses. For example, if Gus reacts badly to loud noises, then we might consider systematic desensitization to reduce his anxiety by decreasing the intensity, frequency, or duration of the noises. Critical to success is the owner's ability to control the dog's environment. Care must be taken not to proceed too quickly and overwhelm the dog. This tool is often used in conjunction with "Improve the Association" (counter-conditioning).

Here are some examples:

- "Gus, I'm sorry you're afraid of sirens. Today, I'll play my siren tape for a little while. It will be so low you'll barely hear it. Tomorrow, I'll turn it up just a little bit. Then, up a bit more, waiting to be sure you're okay with each step."
- "I notice you are not comfortable when large numbers of people are around. Maybe we'll walk over and watch soccer practice tomorrow, but from a distance at first. If you look okay, maybe next time we'll go closer."
- "Gus, you seem to want to keep your distance from the vacuum cleaner when I get it out. Perhaps I won't put it away. I'll leave it in the corner where you can see it without the noise and activity you usually associate with it. If it doesn't bother you, I'll move it closer and closer to the doorway of the kitchen. It will systematically get closer and closer to the door you walk through several times every day."

Take away the reward

Almost all problem behaviors are sustained by a reward of some type. Sometimes the reward is very subtle—you don't see it as a reward, but the dog does. If you can identify the reward with certainty and eliminate it, the behavior will eventually decrease and may stop altogether. The correct term for when an old behavior is eliminated by removing the reward is *extinction*.

Taking away the reward for a problem behavior is easy and takes little time or effort—once you know what that reward is! The problem is that sometimes the reward is not obvious to the owner. Beware! Once you recognize what the rewards are and take them away, the behavior will likely increase immediately! This is known as an *extinction burst*. In plain words, Gus will get worse before he gets better. It might be frustrating, but take it as a good sign. It's working! You've got his number. Stay the course and the behavior will drop off over time.

Here are some examples:

- "Dear, if you stop slipping tidbits to Gus during dinner, begging at the table will stop."

- "Hey Gus, I'll bet you think pulling on the leash is what gets you to the park sooner. From now on when you pull, I'm just going to plant my feet and stand still until the leash goes slack."

- "OK Gus, from now on, the trash is going to be very boring. You will never find table scraps in there again."

- "Gus, when you jump on me I'm going to ignore you because when you are looking for attention my protest antics are actually reinforcing for you."

Take away the reward for jumping up on you. Expect the dog to try harder until he realizes you are not going to pay attention to him when he does that. He will eventually give up.

Reward an incompatible behavior

Probably the most important thing you can do to deal with problem behaviors is to train and reward your dog for another behavior which is incompatible with the inappropriate one. By incompatible, I mean he can't do one behavior (the problem) when he is doing another! The more you reward the incompatible behavior, the stronger it becomes, further reducing the problem behavior. A simple example is to train Gus to sit in cases where he used to jump up. And you do that by making sitting more rewarding to Gus than jumping up.

Rewarding an incompatible behavior reduces stress for all concerned. It does take time to train the new, alternative behavior and you have to be ready to reward it when it's offered or cued. But, once you have accomplished that, it's simply a matter of repetition until the dog knows when and where that behavior is expected. There are lots of appropriate replacement behaviors described in previous chapters.

Here are some examples:

- "You can't chew my shoe and your toy bone at the same time."

- "Here comes a child. 'Gus, Sit.' You can't jump up and sit at the same time. "

- "Instead of barking for joy when Mom comes home, go over to the toy box and pick up a ball. She'll throw it for you. It's more difficult to bark running with a ball in your mouth!"

- "Gus can't annoy us at meal time if he's doing a Down-Stay on his station rug away from the table."

Acclimation

Acclimation is especially helpful to fearful, excitable, or overly reactive dogs. Sometimes referred to as habituation, acclimation simply means getting used to it. The dog is exposed to the problem-producing situation (men in hats, for example) in a safe and controlled manner. The dog should be presented with neither reward nor punishment. Rather a calm and neutral environment will help the frightened dog to discover that there's nothing to fear.

Acclimation is simple. It requires little skill, but it can be time-consuming. With acclimation, one must monitor the situation and stop if the dog is showing signs of stress or you can make matters worse. Keep in mind that when conditioning an individual dog, you are contending with and perhaps going against that dog's instincts. Your success will be impacted by the dog's breed type, individual personality, lifestyle, and reinforcement history.

Acclimation can work with stimuli that the dog sees, feels, hears, or smells. Here are some examples:

- **The look.** "You don't like people in hats? You'll acclimate to hats, because the whole family will be wearing hats when we are around you."

- **The feel.** "Gus, wear this collar please. Get used to it. Nothing bad will happen, nothing good will happen. Period."

- **The sound.** "Gus, I'll have to take you to the boarding kennel next week. I've got a CD of the background music they play in the kennel. Let's play it at home this week."

- **The smell.** "Worried about the vet? Here's a towel that's been in the office. It smells just like the clinic. Get used to it. I'll put it here at home where you have to walk over it each day."

The one tool fix
It's not realistic to think that one single approach will immediately solve a problem. You have lots of options and endless combinations of those options.

Improve the association
Improve the association—more formally known as counter-conditioning—is one of the most widely used and successful behavior modification techniques for overcoming fear and the problem behaviors that may result. It is often used with systematic desensitization (see above). It helps your dog establish a new, acceptable mind set and response to replace the fearful behavior. Improving the association is useful when you can't change the problem environment (you can't get rid of thunderstorms!). The trick is to associate something good with whatever it is that is troubling to the dog. Thunder results in a fabulous treat or the chance to play ball. Simply put, the problem stimulus results in something good. The reward must be strong enough to overcome the problem or you might get the reverse effect—the reward takes on a poor association.

Here are some examples:

- "Gus, I'll bet you'd change your mind about those noisy garbage collectors if I throw a ball for you each time they come."

- "I know he's wearing a white coat and stethoscope, Gus, but he's also got the best liver treats in town."

- "You don't like to ride in the car? (Dog's last three rides were: Groomer, veterinarian, boarding kennel.) Well, this month you'll ride only one block each day—to the park where you can have a lot of fun."

Peanut butter therapy—counter-conditioning in action for a dog who does not like to be brushed.

No need for nasty stuff

This chapter (indeed the entire book) provides humane and effective training alternatives to nasty stuff. What follows is a long list of reasons why you should avoid resorting to punishment and harsh corrections in dog training.

Punishment is an incomplete program

Punishment only addresses what *not* to do. You might get lucky. Your dog might stop the punished behavior…but then what? It's not nice to mug visitors at the door, but is the dog clear on what behavior is expected? Instead, teach him to sit on cue. It's incompatible with jumping!

Punishment can escalate fearful behaviors

While walking, your dog sees a man in a hat. She's worried. She barks at the man and pulls back. You holler and jerk her leash. Now she has to worry about the man *and* you. In addition, she might perceive that you are also reacting to the man, confirming to your dog that the guy really is scary.

Ineffective attempts at punishment can be rewarding and make matters worse
Your dog is in the backyard barking. You open the door and holler, "Bad!" What you consider a punishment, your dog may find rewarding. He saw your face and heard your voice. You *are* paying attention to him. He feels rewarded, regardless of what you are saying.

Using aversives might damage your relationship
My training program is based upon relationship. Punishment can cause confusion and reduces the trust that is so important between you and your dog. It's best to earn your dog's respect by consistency in leadership and good training, not to demand it through intimidation or force.

To be effective, punishment needs to be immediate and consistent
To learn from the consequences of his behavior, the consequence (correction, punishment) should occur within about two seconds of the behavior. Can your timing be that consistent? And the punishment should be experienced every time the problem behavior occurs.

Punishment might not generalize
Your dog sniffed when you asked him to "Heel." You jerk the lead as a correction. In this case, he might think the jerk means no sniffing here, but it's okay to sniff elsewhere. He may not know that you wanted him to Heel! He more likely learned that you are unpredictably mean and grumpy!

Punishment can lead to learned helplessness
The dog decides that no matter what she does, it's wrong, therefore it's safer to do nothing at all. She gives up and just endures the punishment.

Punishment can generate substitute behaviors
Repetitive actions, such as barking, digging, and chewing can calm a dog, much like rocking a baby settles the child. It feels good. If you punish and stop one behavior, she might turn to a substitute behavior for her gratification. The new behavior might be more annoying or dangerous.

The punishment "callus"
Learning theory states that a punishment should be aversive and intense enough to stop the behavior right away. If it is not effective, the tendency is for people to escalate the strength of successive punishments. The resulting "callus" build-up on your dog now requires you to administer a harsher punishment than would otherwise have been necessary before you desensitized your dog.

Where is the line between effective punishment and abuse?
What if your punishment didn't stop or reduce the behavior and you continue the punishment anyway in the name of training. At what point do your actions become

abuse rather than training? The goal of an aversive should be to quickly and permanently change your dog's unwanted behavior. It should not be a means to vent your own frustration.

Now, let's take the remodeling chapter a step further by giving specific examples of good dogs doing bad things and which combination of YESTRAIN tools you might select to address the issue. We can use the common complaint of barking to explore possible options.

The bark stops here

It's normal for dogs to bark and barking is one of the most common behavior problems an owner might face. Chickens cluck, cows moo, dogs bark. Certainly a dog does not view barking as a problem, but too much, too loud, and at the wrong times is a problem—at least for the people who live near the dog.

Barking lends itself well to analysis using the YESTRAIN approach to problem solving. This is because dogs bark for a number of reasons and, because of this, a variety of YESTRAIN techniques may be good options for solving your dog's specific situation. For example, the cause of barking could be one or a combination of the following:

1. Attention seeking   "Will somebody please pay attention to me"

2. Separation anxiety   "Will my special person please come back?"

3. Lack of activity   "I'm bored, barking is my recreation."

4. Excitement   "Do I need a reason? I'm just having a blast."

5. Offensive threat   "I'm bold, I want you out of here and I'll help you go."

6. Defensive alarm   "I'm worried, give me space, let me get out of your way."

Now, let's take a detailed look at a number of case studies and see how you might use the YESTRAIN tools to resolve a variety of barking issues.

Profile of "Libby:" An attention-seeking dog

Libby is a bouncy, cheerful dog who is full of life. She's in the habit of barking for attention from passers-by when Joe, her owner, goes to work and leaves her alone in the yard. Joe is afraid the neighbors will complain. Joe is also concerned with another attention seeking annoyance. When he's on the phone, Libby comes over, stands in front of him and barks. She'll also scratch, scratch, scratch her front paws on the floor just in front of him.

Look-at-me-Libby.

It is readily apparent that Libby wants somebody, anybody, to pay attention. The clue is that Look-at-me-Libby's bark has frequent pauses as she looks to see if anyone is looking. If they do, she might, wag, circle, bow, or look otherwise charming

Take away the reward
Up until the phone rings, Libby is quiet and receives no attention. Once on the phone and trying to have a conversation, Joe attempts to keep Libby quiet by correcting her with the word "Hush." A correction? No, Joe is actually rewarding Libby by looking at and talking to her. Sometimes he even grabs at her to try to settle her down, so now she has an interactive game of keep-away as well.

Acclimate the dog
Libby turns on with the trigger of the ringing phone. Joe could record random phone rings or download ring tones from the internet. He could play them and ignore Libby.

Reward an incompatible behavior
Joe might consider holding back some of Libby's daily ration of kibble and placing it in a food dispensing toy near the phone. He could give her this "pacifier" after the phone rings, but before she starts to bark. Now, instead of looking to Joe for attention, she'll be coaxing the "toy" to give up its bounty.

Profile of "Reno:" A dog suffering from separation anxiety
Separation anxiety is different from attention seeking. A dog wanting attention will settle for any type of general interaction from any person or animal. The anxious dog is overly bonded to one individual. Fortunately these dogs, who suffer greatly when

their person leaves, are in the minority when compared to other types of latchkey dog problems.

Reno and his owner, Jane, live alone. Return-to-me-Reno follows Jane everywhere, even into the bathroom. He barks when Jane leaves him alone and is showing other signs of stress such as drooling and licking his paws. His distress is worse on Mondays and after holidays.

Return-to-me-Reno.

Reno's bark is high pitched and frantic. If we were to set up a video camera we'd see pacing, drooling, whining, scratching, chewing, and howling in the direction Jane was last seen or heard. The anxiety is usually at its worse right after the departure.

Health

Jane could use some ideas on how to begin a stress reduction and enrichment program for Reno. She should also make an appointment to take Reno to the veterinarian.

Can it be OCD?

Sometimes repetitive behaviors are considered obsessive compulsive disorders. An OCD can present itself by certain types of barking, spinning, and licking. "Barker's high" is a self rewarding behavior that makes the dog feel good. The veterinarian might suggest a program of behavior modification and pharmacological intervention, or point you toward other specialists available in your area.

Eliminate the cause or trigger

Because Reno is overly bonded to her, Jane could redirect some of Reno's focus to other people, activities, or toys. Jane should list things Reno enjoys most. The list might include going for a walk, playing fetch, being fed a meal. Jane should then recruit a friend or neighbor to help create a bond with Reno by doing those things with him.

Jane should keep departures non-emotional by leaving quietly without apologies. Upon returning, she should walk in calmly and not greet the dog until later. These subdued arrivals and departures are in an attempt to make the separation less dramatic. Any attention taken away at greetings and departures will be given back at a different time during the day. For at least twenty minutes before a departure, Jane's interactions with Reno should be kept to a minimum, to lessen the blow of Jane's leaving.

Acclimate the dog

Jane might habituate Reno to the departure cues. What alerts Reno that Jane is about to leave? Picking up her briefcase? The jingle of car keys? Putting on her coat? Jane should periodically—when *not* leaving the house—jingle the keys, put her coat on and take it off, carry her purse around the house a bit. She should say nothing while doing so and just ignore Reno.

Systematic desensitization

Jane could systematically desensitize Reno to her departures. She might make a habit of closing the bathroom door behind her to prevent him following her. If she's in the habit of taking him out with her when she collects the mail, leave him behind. Same with taking out the trash. Reno probably knows this is a "quick trip" situation and isn't as apt to get worked up. Jane could start placing a baby gate across a door and keeping Reno on one side for a minute or so, ignoring him. If he's quiet, he should be let out and no fuss made. If he's noisy, wait for a quiet pause, go over and reward, and let him out and ignore him again for a few minutes.

Improve the association

Jane should make Reno look forward to being apart from her. One way is to get the dog hooked on food stuffed toys. She should get out a toy and start paying attention to it. Talk to it, pat it, fill it with food while Reno is watching. Put it on the other side of the room separator where Reno can't reach it. Yes, this is teasing. Jane could then walk around as if she were getting ready for work, picking up her purse, opening the coat closet door. She could return to the toy in a minute or so, admire the toy again, pretend to eat it, all the while ignoring Reno. Then, put Reno and the toy together on the other side of the enclosure and go sit down for a minute or two. End the exercise while Reno is still engaged in the toy by opening the gate and removing the toy. Don't praise him for coming out. The toy rewards him for staying in! A breakthrough has been achieved when Reno's quiet outlasts his interest in the toy.

Profile of "Utah:" A dog who lacks activity

Utah isn't missing people or wanting attention. In human terms, we'd say he's bored. The Under-employed-Utah has lots of time and energy, but nothing to do. Think of a dog's energy level as a whistling tea kettle. The pressure builds up and is then released by a valve. Barking is Utah's release.

Under-employed-Utah sits in one corner of the living room staring into space barking in a monotonous tone. The bark sounds flat and is directed at nothing in particular. The intervals between are consistent, except when embellished with an occasional howl.

Under-employed-Utah.

Management

This is a good case for better management, maybe some first aid measures or lifestyle changes by his owner Lisa. Lisa could research enrichment programs and see if she could get Utah hooked on some latchkey dog hobbies.

Eliminate the cause or trigger

Find something for Utah to do. Some dogs need to be taught to play with toys. Make them come to life for your dog. Pick one up now and then and offer an interactive game. Make them more interesting. Utah had no interest in a cotton rope tug toy which was lying around for months. One night after her dessert was interrupted by a phone call, his owner had the bright idea of spooning some the melted ice cream over the frayed ends of the rope. Utah has been interested ever since in his strawberry chew toy.

Profile of "Elizabeth:" An enthusiastic dog

Elizabeth barks out the windows while she's traveling in the mini van, dashing back and forth barking at things that move. She seems to find that very rewarding. She's "successful" at chasing everything away. Every telephone pole, person, dog, disappears quickly from her view in the car as she is barking. It's annoying and distracting to her owner Raymond. At home, she barks at birds she can see from the sliding glass door. They fly away too. Enthusiastic-Elizabeth has uncontrolled high energy and lots of enthusiasm for life. Things that wouldn't interest another dog arouse her curiosity. She's easily stimulated and lacks impulse control.

Enthusiastic-Elizabeth.

Elizabeth's bark is high pitched and continuous. She's alert, wagging her tail, and panting. She's having a blast.

Eliminate the cause or trigger

Rides would be easier if Elizabeth traveled in a crate draped with a blanket so she couldn't see the things that excite her. Include a toy to pacify her during the ride. At home, Raymond could tape some black construction paper over the lower half of the sliding glass door to cut out Elizabeth's bird viewing station. These ideas would keep Elizabeth from practicing the behavior and buy Raymond some time for training.

Systematic desensitization

Little by little, the blanket and black construction paper could be removed. In the van, open the blanket first toward the front of the car then back. The sides are most stimulating, save them for last.

Take away the reward

Elizabeth gets lots of attention from Raymond when she's barking. "Hey you, shut up." Elizabeth may think Raymond is cheering her on or perhaps joining her in the barking spree. Take that attention away. Reward quiet and calm behaviors instead.

Anti-barking collars

There are a variety of styles. Some produce a shock when the dog barks, some an ultrasonic sound, others a citronella spray. The risk of physical and psychological side effects is great enough to warrant careful research before you consider such a device. Reread the "No need for nasty stuff" section on page 123.

Profile of "Dallas:" A defensive dog

Dallas is troubled when the mailman approaches. He alternatively barks and lunges at the window, then backs up when the man approaches the door. He's very suspicious of the letters which are dropped onto the floor through the slot in the door. Dallas is ill at ease with most people, but he particularly worries about the mailman.

Defensive-threat-Dallas barks a sharp, high-pitched alarm in hopes the scary thing will go away from his threshold point. He might step forward, but then retreats to a "safe" place. Good management would dictate that the owners protect the dog from possible confrontations before and during a fear reduction program.

Defensive-threat-Dallas.

Health

Because fear and stress are can be debilitating to your dog's health, make an appointment with your veterinarian and discuss this behavior. Ask for a referral to someone who specializes in behavior modification.

Eliminate the cause or trigger

A simple first course of action would be to temporarily get a box at the post office and pick your mail up there.

Systematic desensitization

What are the auditory and visual cues that predict the arrival of the mailman? Could it be the sound of the truck and the sight of the uniformed man in a hat climbing the steps. One technique would be for Dallas' owner to obtain a mailman hat. Don't wear it right away, just put it up on a shelf and gradually bring it closer to Dallas. Have family members wear it, then while wearing the hat, the family could play some of the dog's favorite games.

Improve the dog's association

Perhaps Dallas is worried about the fact that the mailman it putting things through the door. Start putting other things through the mail slot. Dog biscuits, rawhide chews, etc. Of course, Dallas will know it's you, but you can graduate to having friends walk up and deliver treats and eventually paper and letters to mimic the mail.

Acclimate the dog

Ask your mailman's cooperation. See if he will put one of your kitchen towels in his delivery truck for a day. Get the scented towel back and make it a place mat under Dallas's food bowl during meals. Dallas might as well start associating the smell of the mailman with something good.

Reward an incompatible behavior

Fortunately, a family member is usually home during delivery time. Dallas loves to fetch, so have his favorite toy ready. Go outside and slip a letter through the slot. Cheerfully rush in and start playing fetch with Dallas. Get a neighbor to deliver some "mail" at the usual delivery times. As soon as Dallas sees someone at the door, or hears the mail slot, start the retrieving before barking starts.

Profile of "Omaha:" An offensive dog

Omaha is a bold, brash dog who growls and barks to protect his food and toys and territory. He has offered inhibited snaps at visitors. He's also in the habit of chasing people and dogs who walk along his property's fence line. He's not so bad on walks, but Omaha's family tends to cross the street when someone else is coming along the sidewalk. He gets along well with his family, has been to training class and responds to cues most of the time, unless too busy chasing off bad guys. Although he's never bitten a person or a dog, his owners live in fear that he'll get over the fence and cause trouble.

Offensive-threat-Omaha.

Offensive-threat-Omaha's bark is often preceded by a growl and escalates into a bark. It's a startling bark of high intensity, but short duration which is great for the shock effect! Self assured, Omaha might carry through with the threat if all the variables are right. A lot of it has to do with critical distance, the imaginary circle around the dog. If a threat crosses the line, Omaha feels something has to be done to get rid of it.

Health

Unlike the previous cases, Omaha is a dog who may engage in dangerously aggressive behavior. If you have a dog like this, you are better off consulting with experts before trying to solve the problem yourself. A good place to start is with your trusted veterinarian or with a referral to someone who understands what makes offensive dogs tick. You want to make sure that there is nothing physically wrong with the dog. In cases where dogs are aggressive and the bark can lead to bites, you have to seek professional help to protect not only your dog but yourself, other people, and other dogs. The course of action will probably include systematic desensitization and rewarding incompatible behaviors. The expert will not only address the outward display, but conditioning a different emotional response to the triggers.

Try management

Until a professional has examined Omaha and recommended the proper course of action, Omaha's owners have to focus on management. Management in this case would focus on keeping Omaha out of situations where he is apt to begin his offensive displays. Avoiding strange dogs and people by crossing the street, which the owners are already doing, is a good first step. Feeding Omaha in a separate closed room, and keeping him confined in a crate when necessary to avoid altercations are also good management strategies.

Think it over

A familiar dictum is, "First, do no harm" many good physicians adopt in their medical practices. This is good advice to enthusiastic and well-meaning dog owners. You should not rush ahead in an attempt to solve a behavior problem without a thorough analysis of the situation and thinking through the possible collateral or long term results of the method used.

This last chapter has given you lots of ideas for replacing inappropriate behavior with acceptable behaviors. It also gives some guidance on thinking through behavior modification concepts. It's just a jump start and it should work for most common behavior problems. If not, contact a behavior and training expert to coach you.

The fewer behavior problems you have, the happier your household will be. And there you have it! Now enjoy your life together!

About the Author

Terry Ryan and her husband, Bill, both work full time for *Legacy Canine Behavior & Training, Inc.,* a school that specializes in reward based dog training methods. They live with their English Cocker Spaniel "Brody." Bill and Terry's daughter is a manager at Boeing and their son is the captain of a coral reef research vessel for NOAA.

Terry has been training and instructing since 1968. She did undergraduate studies in psychology at Washington State University. Terry and her staff teach community classes including puppy head start, pet dog manners and behavior problem consultations. They also conduct continuing education courses such as agility, freestyle, scent work and training games. All of Legacy's instructors are Certified Pet Dog Trainers. Legacy's Training Center on the Olympic Peninsula in Washington hosts several long-term international courses.

Numerous times a year Terry teaches the Karen Pryor Clicker Training Academy, Legacy's Chicken Training Camps I-V and the Terry Ryan instructor's course, "Coaching People to Train Their Dogs." Many of the courses taught at Legacy's Training Center involve training chickens as a science-based exercise in classical and operant conditioning. The students are then taught how to transfer those skills to training dogs. She periodically joins forces with TAG Teach International to conduct corporate team building workshops that include chicken training. Terry has had long-term contracts to create and instruct dog training courses in England and Australia for the Animal Welfare League. Periodically she teaches at several locations in North America, Europe and Asia. She began working with the Samsung Corporation in Seoul, Korea in the fall of 2008. Their human-animal bond division has created a pet dog training class instructor's program. In 2010 Terry began working with the Formosan Animal Assistant Activities Program in Taiwan.

Terry was also the Program Coordinator for the Dean of the College of Veterinary Medicine, Washington State University, from 1981 until 1994. The programs involved the study of the human-animal bond and implementation of animal-assisted therapy programs. She was one of the original members of the Delta Society, an international resource on the human-animal bond and wrote some of Delta's early training literature. From 1997 to 2002, Terry taught ten day behavior courses at American Wildlife Foundation in Indiana, using imprinted wolves as the study subjects.

Terry has maintained membership and held various offices in local, national and international organizations including past president and Life Member of the National Association of Dog Obedience Instructors. She is a charter member of the Association of Pet Dog Trainers. Terry was appointed to the behavior and training advisory board of the American Humane Society in 2010. She was one of six chairpersons who wrote the national standards for humane dog training funded by the American Humane Association in 2002 which was later published at *Guidelines for Humane Dog Training* by the Delta Society. Terry also played a principal role in creating and teaching a national dog training program for the PetSmart chain of pet shops. She has trained and exhibited her own dogs in conformation, obedience, tracking and other dog sports. Terry is an American Kennel Club (AKC) obedience trial Judge Emeritus. Terry was appointed to the behavior and training advisory board of the American Humane Society in 2010.

Terry writes or has written for several national dog magazines including the *American Kennel Club Gazette, Dog Fancy, Off Lead,* and *Clean Run Agility* magazines. In total, she has written over 300 articles on dog training. Her books and booklets include: *Puppy Primer,* 1990; *Leadership Education for Anyone with a Dog,* 1992, 2003; *Games People Play... To Train Their Dogs,* 1995; *Life Beyond Block Heeling,* 1996; *The Toolbox for Remodeling Your Problem Dog,* 1998; *The Bark Stops Here,* 2000; *Outwitting Dogs,* 2004; *Sounds Good* CD series, 2006; T*extbook for instructors: Coaching People to Train Their Dogs,* 2005, 2008. Terry also has a signature series of dog training products available through the Legacy website (www.legacycanine.com).

INDEX

A

acclimation to stress triggers, 126–127, 133–137

aggression. See also defensive behavior; offensive behavior
  in children, 72
  defined, 9
  working toward solutions for, 122

airline crates, 65

alpha roll, 9

ambivalent body language, 13

American Kennel Club Gazette, 141

American Veterinary Society of Animal Behavior, 9

Animal squares game, 78

anthropomorphism, 4

anti-barking collars, 136

anxiety, 126–129. See also separation distress

appeasement signals, 13–14

B

babies, dogs and, 67–68

backyards, 81–82

Bailey, Bob and Marian, 45

balls, 31–32

The Bark Stops Here (Ryan), 141

barking, 17, 81–82, 130–139

baseline posture, 10

bathing, 24

beds, 41

behavior of dogs
  basics of information processing, 2–9
  body language, 10–20
  physical issues and, 21–24

blinking behavior, 14–15

body language
  of dogs, 10–20
  of trainers, 109

bonding between humans and dogs. See relationship building, foundational skills

Boomerang Come exercise, 56–58, 106

boredom, 134–135

boundaries, training for, 48

bowing behavior, 16

buckle collars, 38

BYOD barbecue, 77

C

cafes, dogs and, 80

calming signals, 13–14

capturing a behavior, 46–48, 86

charts for rewards, 26–27

children, dogs and, 67–73

choke collars, 38, 40

Clean Run Agility, 141

clickers, 41, 44–46

Cocker Spaniels, 21

collars
  anti-barking collars, 136
  reaching for, 51–52
  types of, 38–40

Come behavior
  Boomerang Come, 56–58, 106
  Come-When-Called exercise, 106–109
  rewards for, 31

communication
  body language of dogs, 10–20
  between humans and dogs. See relationship building, foundational skills

companionship tapes, 83

conflict avoidance/resolution, 8–9, 10–17, 79–80

From Dogwise Publishing
www.dogwise.com   1-800-776-2665

BEHAVIOR & TRAINING
ABC's of Behavior Shaping. Proactive Behavior Mgmt, DVD set. Ted Turner
Aggression In Dogs. Practical Mgmt, Prevention, & Behaviour Modification. Brenda Aloff
Am I Safe? DVD. Sarah Kalnajs
Barking. The Sound of a Language. Turid Rugaas
Behavior Problems in Dogs, 3rd ed. William Campbell
Brenda Aloff's Fundamentals: Foundation Training for Every Dog, DVD. Brenda Aloff
Bringing Light to Shadow. A Dog Trainer's Diary. Pam Dennison
Canine Body Language. A Photographic Guide to the Native Language of Dogs. Brenda Aloff
Changing People Changing Dogs. Positive Solutions for Difficult Dogs. Rev. Dee Ganley
Chill Out Fido! How to Calm Your Dog. Nan Arthur
Clicked Retriever. Lana Mitchell
Do Over Dogs. Give Your Dog a Second Chance for a First Class Life. Pat Miller
Dog Behavior Problems. The Counselor's Handbook. William Campbell
Dog Friendly Gardens, Garden Friendly Dogs. Cheryl Smith
Dog Language, An Encyclopedia of Canine Behavior. Roger Abrantes
Dogs are from Neptune. Jean Donaldson
Dominance in Dogs. Fact or Fiction? Barry Eaton
Evolution of Canine Social Behavior, 2nd ed. Roger Abrantes
From Hoofbeats to Dogsteps. A Life of Listening to and Learning from Animals. Rachel Page Elliott
Get Connected With Your Dog, book with DVD. Brenda Aloff
Give Them a Scalpel and They Will Dissect a Kiss, DVD. Ian Dunbar
Guide to Professional Dog Walking And Home Boarding. Dianne Eibner
Language of Dogs, DVD. Sarah Kalnajs
Mastering Variable Surface Tracking, Component Tracking (2 bk set). Ed Presnall
My Dog Pulls. What Do I Do? Turid Rugaas
New Knowledge of Dog Behavior (reprint). Clarence Pfaffenberger
Oh Behave! Dogs from Pavlov to Premack to Pinker. Jean Donaldson
On Talking Terms with Dogs. Calming Signals, 2nd edition. Turid Rugaas
On Talking Terms with Dogs. What Your Dog Tells You, DVD. Turid Rugaas
Play With Your Dog. Pat Miller
Positive Perspectives. Love Your Dog, Train Your Dog. Pat Miller
Positive Perspectives 2. Know Your Dog, Train Your Dog. Pat Miller
Predation and Family Dogs, DVD. Jean Donaldson
Quick Clicks, 2nd Edition. Mandy Book and Cheryl Smith
Really Reliable Recall. Train Your Dog to Come When Called, DVD. Leslie Nelson

Right on Target. Taking Dog Training to a New Level. Mandy Book & Cheryl Smith

Stress in Dogs. Martina Scholz & Clarissa von Reinhardt

Tales of Two Species. Essays on Loving and Living With Dogs. Patricia McConnell

The Dog Trainer's Resource. The APDT Chronicle of the Dog Collection. Mychelle Blake (*ed*)

The Dog Trainer's Resource 2. The APDT Chronicle of the Dog Collection. Mychelle Blake (*ed*)

The Thinking Dog. Crossover to Clicker Training. Gail Fisher

Therapy Dogs. Training Your Dog To Reach Others. Kathy Diamond Davis

Training Dogs. A Manual (reprint). Konrad Most

Training the Disaster Search Dog. Shirley Hammond

Try Tracking. The Puppy Tracking Primer. Carolyn Krause

Visiting the Dog Park, Having Fun, and Staying Safe. Cheryl S. Smith

When Pigs Fly. Train Your Impossible Dog. Jane Killion

Winning Team. A Guidebook for Junior Showmanship. Gail Haynes

Working Dogs (reprint). Elliot Humphrey & Lucien Warner

HEALTH & ANATOMY, SHOWING

Advanced Canine Reproduction and Whelping. Sylvia Smart

An Eye for a Dog. Illustrated Guide to Judging Purebred Dogs. Robert Cole

Annie On Dogs! Ann Rogers Clark

Another Piece of the Puzzle. Pat Hastings

Canine Cineradiography DVD. Rachel Page Elliott

Canine Massage. A Complete Reference Manual. Jean-Pierre Hourdebaigt

Canine Terminology (reprint). Harold Spira

Breeders Professional Secrets. Ethical Breeding Practices. Sylvia Smart

Dog In Action (reprint). Macdowell Lyon

Dog Show Judging. The Good, the Bad, and the Ugly. Chris Walkowicz

Dogsteps DVD. Rachel Page Elliott

The Healthy Way to Stretch Your Dog. A Physical Therapy Approach. Sasha Foster and Ashley Foster

The History and Management of the Mastiff. Elizabeth Baxter & Pat Hoffman

Performance Dog Nutrition. Optimize Performance With Nutrition. Jocelynn Jacobs

Positive Training for Show Dogs. Building a Relationship for Success Vicki Ronchette

Puppy Intensive Care. A Breeder's Guide To Care Of Newborn Puppies. Myra Savant Harris

Raw Dog Food. Make It Easy for You and Your Dog. Carina MacDonald

Raw Meaty Bones. Tom Lonsdale

Shock to the System. The Facts About Animal Vaccination... Catherine O'Driscoll

Tricks of the Trade. From Best of Intentions to Best in Show, Rev. Ed. Pat Hastings

Work Wonders. Feed Your Dog Raw Meaty Bones. Tom Lonsdale

Whelping Healthy Puppies, DVD. Sylvia Smart

Dogwise.com is your source for quality books, ebooks, DVDs, training tools and treats.

We've been selling to the dog fancier for more than 25 years and we carefully screen our products for quality information, safety, durability and FUN! You'll find something for every level of dog enthusiast on our website www.dogwise.com or drop by our store in Wenatchee, Washington.